SUPER DUPER PROFITABLE ADS

Swipe My $5 Video Ads Playbook That Grew My Consulting Business To 7+Figures

By: Laurel Portie

FOREWORD

It is impossible to overlook the extent to which thoughtful and extraordinary people have an impact on our lives…

Especially if that person is Laurel Portie.

I am biased… like a proud uncle. She never ceases to amaze me and make me grateful that someone like her is in my life. Her energy is infectious, and her generosity and dedication are inspiring.

Laurel came into my life as a client through The Network with Nic Peterson and Dan Giulianotti in 2019.

From the first day, I was impressed with how she lived and did her business on her own terms. I also dug the fact that in her career, she wrote the sizzle lines to entice television viewers to stay up for the 11 o'clock news… ***"Man bites dog. Film at 11!"***

Before she came to The Network, all the gurus she had met with had told her that her business model was wrong and that having a $7.00 per month program teaching EVERYTHING about running ads that generate sales profitably was WAY TOO CHEAP… that she was leaving money on the table.

For us, we thought what she was doing was incredible and totally in sync with her values.

Laurel is on a mission… to help as many entrepreneurs succeed as possible, and she did not want finances to be the limiting factor. Her $7.00 per month program is just one example of her dedication and generosity, but it is undoubtedly the most demonstrative.

For Laurel to call me one of her mentors is a great honor, but all I ever did was hold up a mirror and let her see what she was doing and what it meant to her clients, their businesses, and the people they serve.

Laurel has a way about her that is as disarming as it is inspiring. I saw this firsthand when she worked with my wife on her College Prep Counseling business. Before Laurel, my wife felt like a fish out of water with *"all this ad stuff.,"* but Laurel made her feel so comfortable and confident that she is now working her ads, funnels, and engagement like an old pro.

Her dedication to meeting her clients where they are, encouraging them to elevate their minds, and guiding them with the tools and simple methodology to achieve measurable and sustainable results is a masterclass in leadership and instruction.

Laurel takes her business and community very seriously… and all she expects in return (besides $7.00 per month) is that her clients also take their business seriously.

Laurel is one of the most thoughtful people I know, but if you expect her to work with you and hold you accountable for your success habits, you better pull your Big Boy or Girl pants on because she is the real deal.

Laurel wants her clients to succeed so badly that I think she gets frustrated because sometimes it seems as if she cares more about her clients' success than they do. Not to say that her clients don't want to be successful… but maybe they are not as dedicated to doing what they need to do to BE successful.

If there is only one thing I know, it's that Laurel will never give up on a client… even long after the client seems to have given up on themselves. She knows that what she teaches works. Not just because it has worked for her but because she has seen it work for thousands of clients in her community.

I can go on and on about Laurel… like a proud uncle.

One of the great things about knowing someone like Laurel is that she is easy to refer to friends and other business associates. Every time I have introduced her to someone, "I" end up looking like a hero because she has such an impact on them that it feels like I presented them with a beautiful gift… because I did.

So, this Foreword has been my introduction of Laurel to you. You're welcome. ●

In this book, Laurel lays out the entire blueprint, roadmap, or whatever you want to call it to be able to produce Super Duper Profitable Ads for your business on autopilot so you can do what you love, thrive in what you do, and prosper in your business so you can live life on your terms.

The only thing I will warn you about is after you read this book and do what it guides you to do, you will have an insatiable appetite for more Laurel.

Don't fret… Laurel will be there for you.

Read this book. Consume it. Digest it. Most importantly, USE IT. You will be forever grateful that you did.

To Your Success,

Jeff Moore

Director, Global Protein Group
Founder, Thursday Night Boardroom

CONTENTS

INTRODUCTION

If we ever get to meet in person, you'll notice something about me right away -- I'm pretty short. And growing up, that put me at a distinct disadvantage on the basketball court... or so it would seem.

Every time I went for a layup or tried driving to the basket, I would get shut down. I learned early on that if I was going to score some legit points, I needed a new approach. So I decided to become insanely good at shooting free throws so I could slowly rack up points for my team.

Not the sexiest strategy, but it worked!

It turned out that by playing the "slow game," scoring one point at a time, those little bits would accumulate to a lot of points over time. It was the relentless application of the basics.

Fun fact, I even won the Louisiana State Free Throw Championship a few years in a row.

If you've been scoping out the online coaching, consulting and service provider space at any point in the past few years, you've likely noticed a trend…

It seems everyone has a cool "new" trendy strategy or process that they promise will make you millions of dollars with no effort. All you have to do is post an ad that directs folks to your brilliantly crafted webinar or workshop and you will magically achieve 10x ROAS (that's Return on Ad Spend).

In other words, the exact opposite of the slow game.

The highly scripted and painfully unoriginal messaging goes something like this:

"Running ads is like a money printing machine… For every dollar you put in, you get two dollars back." And then of course this is followed by a screenshot of their ads manager dashboard where they show you these incredible numbers.

But here's the thing.

That mentality is one dimensional and incredibly fragile.

It doesn't account for the most important variable that determines whether or not your business will succeed or not -- how people actually make decisions.

We'll get into that more later- But first, a quick slice of my own life and business, so you can see how shifting your perspective will get you what you want without the fragility of the typical model you see everywhere else.

I didn't get my start in the world of internet marketing. In fact, I started out in the world of television, and one of my most daunting tasks was to create simple and quick messaging that would prompt people to watch the 11 o'clock news.

This was no easy task.

I'll share the details in chapter 3 of how I managed to navigate that challenge. I've taken all that I learned about influence and marketing from that world, added some extra bits I picked up along the way, and condensed the strategy inside these pages.

The results?

On Sep 21st, 2021 my business hit the $1M mark …. with just under $37,000 in ad spend.

"Laurel, are you trying to tell me you got almost 28x ROAS?!"

Yes, but not in the conventional way that you see splattered all over the internet.

In fact, when you look at my ads manager, the average displayed ROAS is just 51 **CENTS** per dollar spent.

You might think, "so wait, your ads lost money?"

Not exactly.

Remember, you have to stop thinking one dimensionally and open your mind to a completely new paradigm.

And if you stick with me, I'll walk you through the ecosystem that I used to create a multi-million dollar business leveraging a few simple videos that I run as $5 ads.

Will you get the same results?

We'll never know until you put this system into play.

But I can tell you that after working with over 10,000 coaches and service providers, there is one thing that sets apart the successful from the wannabees -- relentless application of the basics.

And if you put this strategy into play, I'll show you how to hit as many free throws in your business as you want to.

I EVEN HAVE A FREE THROW LINE & BASKET IN MY OFFICE TO REMIND ME ... OR IT'S JUST TO HAVE FUN IN BETWEN CLIENT CALLS ☺

So let's get into it!

CHAPTER 1

A SWIFT KICK IN THE PANTS

"Most people prefer the certainty of misery to the misery of uncertainty."

— Virginia Satir

I can still vividly remember my first coaching call with my mentor Nic Peterson. I was specifically looking for someone who could validate that the $7/month ads program I had started was a good idea.

Deep in my gut, I knew I was on track with my $7/month ads program, but everyone in the coaching space was poo-pooing the idea.

In fact, I had been in conversation with another popular online guru at the time who had encouraged me to let go of my $7/month ads program and focus on "high-ticket" exclusively.

For context, this was back in 2018 when big box coaching programs were all the rage pushing their high-ticket frameworks into the business space. Every coach and consultant felt the pressure to launch high-ticket, which also saturated the market.

With this being the case, I wanted to zig, when everyone else wanted to zag. Not everyone can afford a high-ticket program, so what happens to them? Could I help them? I saw an opportunity with this untapped market.

But luckily, a good friend of mine, Brandon Hofer, suggested I talk to this Nic guy to get some clarity on how I could make this low-ticket idea of mine work. And it was in that chat that something finally clicked -- I was on the right track, and would embrace going against the grain of what was trendy at the time.

You know what I mean, it's those trendy little tricks that so many gurus promise will somehow instantaneously inject jet fuel into your business and boost you to glory. So many people wanted to sell me the magic bullet and push me into their framework and one-dimensional approach.

Nic was the first person I talked to in the business world that told me I was on the right track with my $7/month program because I was targeting an audience of people that all of the high ticket gurus were completely ignoring. I was filling a gap in the marketplace and he would help me figure out a strategy to do nothing else but get as many people into that program as possible.

I was excited, but uncertain that I'd have what it takes to scale that sort of business model.

Over the 4+ years that I've worked with Nic, there has been a recurring quote that has really hit home for me. I know a lot of you guys are thinking...

"If I execute everything that Laurel is telling me to do inside this book will I be able to grow my coaching business to 7 figures? Is it certain?"

We're all adults here, so I'll be upfront with you -- just simply owning and reading this book will not grow your business.

But take a pause and reflect on this quote that Nic always refers me back to over and over again.

"Most people prefer the certainty of misery to the misery of uncertainty."

Many of you who read this book will hesitate to take action, because you're not certain of the outcome - and you may even be subconsciously hunting for that elusive "magic bullet." The temptation will be to stay where you are right now in your business because it feels comfortable and familiar.

In other words, you may prefer the misery of staying where you are -- buying more courses and always "getting ready" to execute -- because you're uncertain of what the outcome would be if you took the plunge and did something very different than the norm.

And look, there's no judgements from me. I'm simply here to help you take those first big steps so you don't have to stay stuck in that uncertainty.

Bottom line is, this **WILL** work if you implement the process consistently. You just need a plan that works.

Which is what you're reading right now.

If you keep standing on the sidelines and waiting for the "certain" thing, you'll end up creating the exact opposite outcome than what you're truly after. (Or worse yet, you'll fall for one of the "magic bullet" programs).

The reality is, those of you who are uncertain of what will happen if you invest your money into advertising will express that uncertainty through hesitation.

And then that hesitation gets you more of what you've always gotten.

So let's just agree from the get-go: feeling uncertain can be disorienting. But not as disorienting as staying where you are.

Along the way, I'm going to help you alleviate some of that uncertainty, but when the time comes, you'll need to take the plunge and as Steven Pressfield says, "do the work."

ACTION SATISFACTION

Not long ago, one of my brand new students in my $7/month ads program wrote a massively long and detailed post in the private Facebook group, documenting her past experience with other ad programs and how she just couldn't get it to work for her.

She wanted to know if this program was "certain." In other words, will this work for me?

And look, I get it. Sometimes people just need a good ol' fashioned venting session and need to feel heard and validated.

But I'm not Laurel the Life Coach over here, and I couldn't help but roll my eyes a bit at the thought of someone spending that much time and effort cataloging their past failures, when they literally could have used the exact same amount of time executing the first ad strategy and field testing their messaging to get a real result!

Here's my point -- if you will agree ahead of time to put your energy into executing the process, rather than focusing on everything that hasn't worked in the past, you will be shocked at how well this works.

In fact, my Lean on Laurel program has a near 100% success rate for those who execute a series of simple actions.

Now the good news! The strategies that I will walk you through step by step inside this book were built to rig the game in your favor. That means you'll be able to execute with the least amount of risk (and money) as possible.

I promise that you will save thousands of hours (and dollars!) by following the leveraged approach in these pages. I'll show you $2 and $5 ads that attract your ideal client faster and easier, without having to chase them down using organic strategies on social media.

SATURATION VS. COMPETITION

One of the biggest mental roadblocks my students express when applying my strategies is that market saturation is to blame when they aren't getting the momentum they want.

But let's unpack this a bit, because this will make or break you.

Even the market I serve looks super saturated from the outside. I mean, really, have you seen how many "programs" are out there that promise to teach you ads?

And yes, it's true, the coaching space has become quite active lately, with a lot of voices that all appear on the surface to be promising similar outcomes.

And in the past few years, there has been a flood of coaching programs that teach people that they can sell their expertise by packaging it up into a high-ticket offer. Five years ago anyone could run paid traffic to that offer and become a multimillionaire with ease.

But times have changed… and that's a good thing!

There are more courses being created every single day than there used to be in an entire year.

So yes, the market is becoming more and more saturated, but there's actually very little competition.

Let me explain what I mean by that.

Your audience is seeing a ton of online coaching offers every single day, but their marketing efforts and offers fall short, cutting them out as competition. This leaves massive opportunity to those who know how to master just three things:

1. Creating content that will attract your ideal audience
2. Using ads to put that content in front of that audience
3. Having conversations with that audience to help solve their problems

For the first two and a half years of my business, I had mastered #1 and #3.

I didn't want to dive into #2, because I saw the amount of money some of the most successful internet gurus were putting into the ads platform (I ran a lot of their ads, so I had an insider perspective).

So I decided I was going to depend on organic marketing only, and it cost me hundreds (if not thousands) of hours of time with my family.

It wasn't until my mentor Nic taught me how to take risks by playing my own game that things really clicked. I was an ad expert for some of the industries most successful coaches, so I knew how to make big budgets work to make them millions of dollars.

I even won this award for building seven figure ad strategies in the online coaching industry…

But I was uncertain if I could take those same skills and apply them with a much smaller budget.

Could it yield the same results for a small business like mine? He challenged me to step into the risk of uncertainty and it provided me with an enormous upside.

Are you willing to do the same?

CHAPTER 2
MAGIC MATH

If you're looking to scale your coaching business to $10k+ a month and beyond, you are going to love this book. I have written it as a playbook filled with strategies and tactics that you can immediately implement. Strategies that will stand the test of time.

My client Scott used the methods I'll outline in this book to create an amazing lifestyle business in which he works around 2 to 3 hours per day and consistently pulls in $11,000 per month... with just $500/month in ad spend! (more on that approach later on)

"Wait Laurel, what if I want to scale to $50,000 a month, will this still work?"

Yeah, but the actual number is totally up to you, which is what makes this strategy so cool!

MOST of my students choose to live a super chill lifestyle, but there are some of my students who have scaled their business to 6-figure months utilizing this same framework with a little help from a virtual assistant or two.

I'll put my own money where my mouth is. I've made over 2 million dollars over the last 5 years using the exact same strategies outlined in this playbook and I still use these strategies today.

Bottom line is, the strategies here put **YOU** in the driver's seat.

I'm going to show you a consistent and profitable way to run Facebook or YouTube ads without needing to hire a media buyer or an expensive ad agency. Plus, you won't need any expensive camera equipment, or an existing audience to sell to.

Still skeptical? That's okay. There are so many silly gurus out there preaching so many conflicting messages, it can be challenging to find the voice among the many that gives you a clear path forward.

And I get it, right now you might be thinking, "I can't run Facebook and YouTube ads by myself… don't I need to spend my kids' college fund to hire one of those fancy agencies?"

The short answer to that is… absolutely not.

The mechanics of running ads is a lot easier than you think -- but we can't jump into the mechanics too soon or the whole house falls apart.

So before we dive into the actual nuts and bolts of the ad strategy and how it works, we've got to get our foundations set first.

When new students jump into my $7/month program to learn all about the implementation of this strategy, I see a recurring theme among many of them -- they want to jump right into the button clicking of ads manager because they think that's where the magic sauce is.

The mechanics of ads manager is so simple that I can teach a fifth grader how to push the buttons on a seven figure ad account right now and they will get the same results that I would!

Crazy, right?

I know this because some of my private clients pay their own kids to push the buttons inside their ads manager while they take that free time to create solid content and laser targeted messaging.

As we discussed before, there are only three things we need to master in order to use paid ads to grow your coaching business.

1. Creating content that will attract your ideal audience
2. Using ads to put that content in front of the right audience
3. Having conversations with that audience to help solve their problems

So, if the mechanics of running your own ads is really this easy, why do so many big agencies with major credibility **FAIL** to be successful with running ads for small businesses like yours and mine?

I have found that it all boils down to one thing…

Most big agencies are not using strategies that will build up their clients' authority.

Let me explain it this way:

Let's say that my agency takes on Oprah as a client, and she is selling the hottest weight loss technique that uses bread as its secret weapon. (this is already better than any other ad campaign I've ever seen!)

Let's also say my agency takes you on as a client and you have the exact same offer as Oprah. (where is everybody getting this magic bread?)

Theoretically, I could build the exact same ad strategy for both clients using the same ad budget, but who do you think will sell more programs in the first 90 days?

Oprah of course!

She has built up her name and her brand for decades! She already has authority in the marketplace. You, on the other hand, need more time to establish yourself as an authority to that same audience.

Part of that authority comes from speaking clearly and powerfully to the "gap" that your clients are feeling deeply even before you talk to them. More on the "gap" in a bit.

The first strategy I'm going to show you in this book will accelerate your credibility so that you can win over more clients with a short amount of time.

But first, I just want to be clear that success with advertising is **NOT** what you think.

Most people think success from advertising comes from pushing certain buttons and then looking at the data that the ads manager spits out on a weekly basis, but that is the wrong data to look at.

"Laurel, do you mean all those cool screenshots I see splattered all over the interwebs are misleading?"

Yes and yes.

And by the way, even if the only thing you take away from reading this book is the idea that you need to look beyond the one-dimensional data that most silly gurus hype up, then it will have been worth your time.

We need to dig deeper than the data that is in your ads manager.

I am going to teach you the correct data to track in order to get an accurate picture of how your coaching business is doing when it comes to advertising. Only then will you be able to get results like Scott's where $500/month in advertising leads to 5-figure months.

I want you to take a look at the screenshot below.

This screenshot is straight out of my Facebook ads manager on the exact day my business hit my first seven-figures.

On the left you can see that I spent almost $37,000 in order to hit that number. On the right is Facebook telling me how much I am getting back for every dollar that I've spent advertising on their platform.

According to Facebook, with every dollar I'm putting in, I'm losing half of it!

So if I'm profitable, then why does Facebook think that I'm losing money?

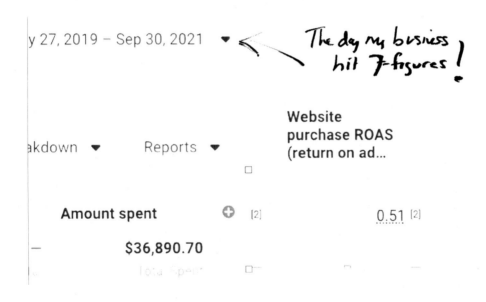

It's because Facebook is only tracking the direct engagement that came from the ad. It's not tracking every action that happens after a person sees an ad.

The data Facebook provides can be misleading and discouraging to those who don't understand the *"Magic Math"* that I will explain in this chapter. Just this morning, one of my private clients was about to fall victim to that data.

She blew up my messenger this morning concerned that she only got one booked call from her latest ad on Facebook. I said, okay, let's break this down.

"How many total calls have you gotten this week?"

"Eight" she said.

I asked her, "Okay, where did the other seven that aren't being tracked by the ads manager come from?"

"Oh, I talked to them in messenger over the last few days."

"That's awesome" I said.

Then asked "So, where did they find out about you?"

She said, "oh, they saw my ad a few months ago on…"

She didn't even finish the sentence. She knew what I was going to say.

Facebook may have only tracked one booked call because *that* conversion happened on the ads platform within the last 7 days, but the other 7 happened in messenger because they saw her ad months ago, started following her, saw her content consistently over the last few weeks and were now finally ready to take action. They didn't book through her ad, they went to her messenger to ask questions before they booked.

I'm telling you this because this happens all the time.

People think their ads aren't effective because of Facebook's lack of attribution data.

But, that's enough about ads for now. You need to understand the foundational strategy I used to get the *"Magic Math"* that is the key to your success with this strategy.

A QUICK BACKSTORY

I think it would be a huge disservice if I didn't outline my own framework that got me to my first six figures. The reason is because I want you guys to see that I am nothing special.

The way that I stumbled across this awesome strategy was because I focused on one number and one number only.

Let me explain how this all happened.

For almost two decades I worked for some of the largest television companies in the entire world. I started the journey in 2002 long before social media was actually a thing.

In 2008, my boss at the television station asked if I would help them set up a Facebook account to see if that would bring in more viewers. I'm laughing as I'm typing this because he followed that statement with saying, "this will likely be a waste of your time but I think it will be a fun experiment for you."

What ended up happening was that social media became the biggest competitor for my television company.

The TV station down the street was no longer the biggest threat to my company's success, their biggest competitor was now the smartphone in people's hands that are hogging their attention while they're sitting in front of the TV.

Here is where the main part of my signature strategy was born.

I had to figure out a way to pull viewers right out of their social media feed and to pay attention to the content that was being put out by my television company I was working for.

I developed a two-tier ad strategy where I ran $5 video ads.

Tier One was made up of evergreen branding messaging that would sell viewers on why they should watch my station's newcast every night, versus reading the news on their smartphone.

Tier Two was made up of specific episodic messaging promoting stories that were coming up that week.

Right now, all you need to understand about those two tiers is that I was sending tier one to a cold audience, meaning they had never engaged with my TV station's Facebook page before.

Tier two was being sent to people who had already engaged with our Facebook page.

I am a very visual person, so I want you to get a real picture of what this looks like drawn out.

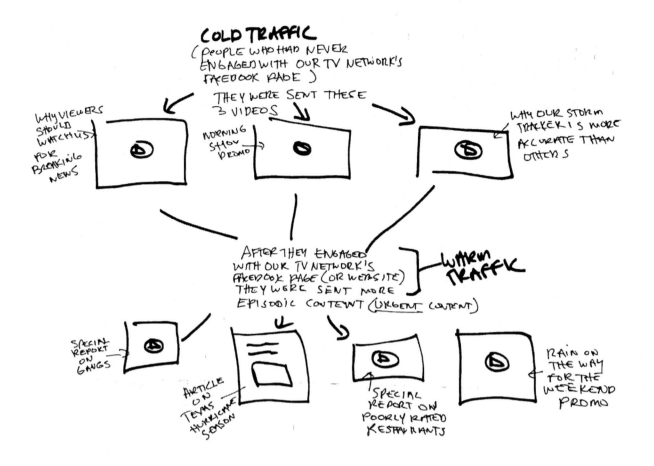

You can likely see where this is going, but for now, I only want you to keep in mind there are two tiers in the strategy I am running for my TV station.

This ad strategy I had developed, landed me some pretty sweet gigs at various TV stations across the country, but it wasn't until I got hired by a TV show that filmed each day in Phoenix, AZ that I met my wife, that everything changed.

A few months into our dating, she told me that she wanted to start a t-shirt company. I was like, that's cool. I know nothing about that, but let's just jump right in. We did, and we did pretty good. It wasn't anything we could quit our jobs over, but we were starting to get some traction.

In case you're wondering, our niche targeted women cyclists and our t-shirts were fun and cheeky. We struggled to find fun bicycle t-shirts in women's styles, so we decided to fill that gap. There's that word, gap, again. We'll definitely dig more into that.

Long story short, we ended up at a Daymond John workshop with our very own business consultant who was supposed to be helping us scale our t-shirt brand, but he was more impressed with my Facebook ad skills so he took our consulting session in another direction.

"I don't know why we're sitting here talking about t-shirts, you have a much more valuable skill Businesses will pay you a lot of money to run their ads for them."

He told me exactly how much more and it was 12X the amount each month I was making at the TV station. I was skeptical, but I decided to put his statement to the test.

THE MATH PROBLEM THAT GOT ME TO MY FIRST 6-FIGURES

The sexy thing to do when you start your own business is "stick it to the man" and just go "all in" and grind 24/7. But I had bills to pay and a new wife to take care of. So that was not going to be the path I wanted to start my new life with my wife on.

Instead, I carved out a simple math problem. If I didn't hit my numbers, I'd forget about this silly idea that I got from "workshop guy," and I'd continue to live the glamorous life of a TV producer.

The math?

Make enough to pay my rent and my bills, which in downtown Phoenix was roughly about $3,000 a month. That doesn't sound like much, but when you are making zero, that sounds like a great place to start.

It was realistic and it was a test. I still had my full time job as my safety net but it was also a liability because I didn't have a lot of time to get this business going so I knew I had to be strategic with my time.

Would businesses *really* pay me to help them grow using the strategy I was using for the various Television companies throughout the years?

There was only one way to find out, I had to find a way to have conversations with those business owners.

The initial math was easy. If I needed to make $3,000/month to pay for my bills, I needed to bring in 6 clients each at $500/month.

$3K/Month = 6 ad clients at $500/month

The next math problem was an equation I needed to solve, but once I had the data, it would be easy to solve over and over again.

How many people do I need to talk to in order to sell 6 of them into my ad services?

The equation:

Talk to _____ people = 6 ad clients

I created a strategy that revolved around the 2 things I knew best… video and talking to people. One thing that I learned from some of the best sales people in the television advertising industry is that conversations are the fastest path to cash. I'll say that again in bold, because it's a super important concept that not a lot of people take advantage of.

CONVERSATIONS ARE THE FASTEST PATH TO CASH.

Let's unpack that for a minute.

If conversations are the fastest path to cash, why do so many coaches and consultants build huge, elaborate funnels that put so much friction in between them and their ideal clients?

That was a concept I never understood.

So while all my competitors who wanted to do ads for business owners spent time and money building funnels, I focused on a simple strategy that would bring me face to face with my ideal clients, faster and with the least amount of friction.

I made it my goal to talk to 100 business owners over a zoom call over the next 90 days and I was going to lure them in with Facebook live videos. The only problem…

I needed to figure out how to get these videos in front of those business owners.

The video that started it all ♡

Over the next week, I went **LIVE** on Facebook every single day and I found local chamber groups who would allow me to post my videos as long as I didn't promote my services, which was cool… But, how will I make money if I can't promote?

What I started doing was just adding a whole bunch of business owners as friends.

AHA! I thought…Surely the requests for me to hop on a free zoom call with them would start piling in as soon as they started seeing my content.

Cue Sad Trombone

That wasn't the case at all. My videos were hardly being seen by anyone.

I had to figure out a way for my videos to get **MORE** reach, **MORE** engagement and most importantly... more **conversations** with business owners.

I noticed a strategy that was very popular at the time by multi-level marketers. They called them "comment ladders." They would ask people if they wanted to see how they could work from home and make a "gazzilion dollars."

The comments came pouring in on every single post I saw.

That got me thinking... what if I used the same concept in my videos?

If I gave something away of value during my live video... would my ideal clients comment to get it so that my video would get more reach, and most importantly, more engagement?

Sure enough.

Within just 7 days, my videos were getting 50+ comments of business owners wanting everything from advertising checklists to strategy, and they even started raising their hands for a free strategy session.

Laurel Portié was live.

June 29, 2018 · 🌐 ▾

FB Ads Quickfire Lesson!

☑ PPE, Traffic or Conversion?

☑ The one thing businesses get wrong when they're running fb ads.

Apply for a FREE strategy call with ME >> http://bit.ly/CallWithLaurel

❤👍 19   24 Comments 10 Shares 361 Views

I was finally starting to get some traction. Every morning I woke up at 5am and went live. I took free strategy calls during my lunch hour and then planned my next day's content. The entire process took me about 3 hours a day on top of my normal day job.

I'm telling you this because I am no one special. I didn't have any extra time in my day. I created a math problem that I could easily solve with the right strategy. It wasn't perfect. Most of the time I rolled outta bed with bad hair, but I was disciplined in my simple little strategy.

Everyday I planned my videos, added business owners as friends and consistently went live.

But it wasn't until later that summer, when I applied a little copywriting framework that took my video strategy to the next level, that I quickly hit my 100 zoom call goal. Booking myself out with Facebook ad clients who were looking for a more budget-friendly strategy.

A little nuance you may have missed in my story… I only focused on one number. That was getting 100 Zoom calls with ideal clients.

Here is a visual recap of what I did for those 90 days.

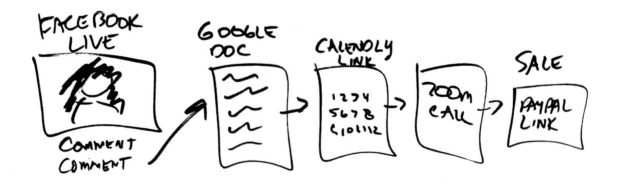

Step 1. I went LIVE on Facebook, teaching an ads tactic or strategy.

Step 2. I asked people to comment for a free checklist/cheat sheet that I now call a "value bomb"

Step 3. I reached out to everyone who had commented in messenger and asked them a few questions to help them diagnose an ads problem they were currently having.

Step 4. I proposed a free ad audit with everyone, while giving them the checklist or cheat sheet they were asking for under my LIVE video.

Step 5. I had free 15-20 minute zoom calls with people who booked.

Step 6. I sent everyone who asked to work with me a paypal link.

The steps above are actually a sales funnel, it's just not the typical sales funnel that most gurus talk about. That exact sales funnel made me my first and second six figures and didn't cost me a dime.

People make excuses that they don't have "this or that" and that's why they aren't successful, but the secret to success really depends on 2 things.

1. Being specific in your goal and having a measurable number attached to that goal.

2. Only doing the activities that lead to that goal over and over again.

I did the same exact things for 90 days, over and over again. When something didn't work, I optimized it and tried it again. I didn't change my goal, nor did I change the specific activity. I focused on optimizing the activity that I was doing, over and over again until I got the result I wanted.

Because of the 90 days of consistency, I now have data that reveals a winning formula that I can replicate again and again.

MAGIC MATH

I went back and counted every post, every comment and every messenger conversation that led to getting those 100 zoom calls.

Here's where the magic math comes into play after 90 days of data. I can now fill in **ALL** the blanks in this math problem.

I need _____ zoom calls to sell 6 people.

I need _____ messenger conversations to get on _____ zoom calls.

I need _____ comments to get _____ messenger conversations.

I need _____ posts to get _____ comments.

After knowing this data, I highlighted the types of posts that led to the most comments and only did those types of posts the following month.

I was able to get 4X the amount of business owners reaching out to me by doing **FEWER** posts.

I have repeated that same math equation every quarter. Now, with reliability, I can repeat those same actions again and again and get the same, if not better results every single time because I am optimizing to get more conversations with less work.

The process sounds simple, but it's not easy.

I always tell my students, if you can consistently do this every 90 days, the *"magic math"* will continue to work in your favor. The problem is that most people are too lazy to track the data or they want results *FASTER*.

Remember this.

It's not 90 days to success *(as most gurus will promise…)* **it's 90 days to data.**

After I achieved my "magic math" problem, I optimized (did more of the things that worked) the heck out of it the following 90 days and got even *BETTER* results.

Good news for those of you who are reading this book. There's a much faster way to get the data you need.

Little did I know… The answer to accelerating this *ENTIRE* process that took me from zero to my first (and second) six figures, was sitting right in front of me, the whole time.

I was teaching it to everyone, but neglecting to use this little accelerator myself.

WHOMP WHOMP

Are you ready to learn my secret formula to putting this powerful $5 ad together?

Let's get to work!

CHAPTER 3

WHY THIS STRATEGY WORKS

As you get deeper and deeper into this strategy, you'll notice it boils down to three very simple and straightforward principles:

1. Content
2. Consistency
3. Conversations

But don't mistake that simplicity to mean that it's easy. It is rather you practicing your "free throws" every day, putting into action the process that will push your business to the next level.

I'm not shy about bragging about my clients and the results they've gotten with this approach. In fact, inside our Lean on Laurel community, we have a nearly 100% success rate! How is that possible? Simple… those who implement this strategy win every time, without exception.

If you go back and take a quick glance at the table of contents for this book, you'll see it's really about breaking down just those three principles.

I'm going to give you the anatomy of your Content, show you how to use it to create Conversations, then give you a step by step action plan so you can show up Consistently as a source of authority for your audience.

My students build their content strategy around what we call *"Power Content."* That means they create content centered around their methodology, with a very structured approach.

It's also the approach I used in my business, even when the so-called gurus in this space made fun of me very directly and told people that I was a phony and that they were wasting their money doing business with me.

In fact, I even lost some great clients to some of these gurus because they were telling these clients that my strategy would **not** work because I wasn't running conversion campaigns. I can't help but laugh about it now because the exact strategy they said wouldn't work is **the** reason I'm still standing today when so many of them fell off the face of the internet from lack of real results.

In this chapter, I want to break down a few nuances of the strategy and explain why it works so well. Because even if you have the perfect strategy, it will be tempting to throw in the towel after a month or two when the guru-types start popping up and telling you you're doing it wrong and to follow them instead.

If you understand why this approach is so powerful, you'll be able to stick it out for the long haul, even in the face of the haters.

LEVELING THE PLAYING FIELD

So why does this strategy work so well? In my experience, there are a few subtle nuances that most people miss when it comes to implementation.

They miss them because they are so focused on the strategies that the gurus are pitching, but neglect to realize these gurus have massive ad budgets that beginning businesses just can't replicate.

Most of the ad strategies those gurus are pitching won't work for people like you and me.

I had to come up with a way that would make ads more affordable for **EVERYONE** to have a chance to play in the marketing game.

I thought to myself, if **MOST** marketers are using conversion campaigns, is there a way I can utilize the video view campaigns? After all, that's what I was using to get more viewers for my TV station.

I wanted to **reach the same audience**, but **for a cheaper cost** while getting a higher quality client over time.

And this is where my video ads ecosystem was born. Let me explain the elements that make this work so well.

PROLIFIC CONTENT - The first nuance of this strategy is publishing **"prolific"** content. This is longer form content that gives your prospect the clarity they need in order to move forward.

A question I get asked a lot is…

"Laurel, can I just do 60 second videos? Those are so much easier to do."

There is a place in my strategy for 60 second videos but right now I need you to understand the importance of putting out longer form videos, or "prolific" content.

There are two primary reasons people **don't** buy. The first is they don't know what they will actually get when they purchase. Makes sense, right? Would you buy anything if you weren't 100% certain on what you'd get after transferring your dollars to another person?

And the second reason people don't buy is that they aren't convinced they should buy specifically from you in the midst of a competitive market with dozens if not hundreds of other options.

Your prolific content gives you the chance to go deeper on your unique mechanism and frameworks. This helps your audience get clarity on how **YOU** can help them.

I know 60 second videos are easier, but they don't allow the space for anyone to get the clarity they need to move forward – at least not in the way that most people are doing them. That's a little teaser for what's coming in a later chapter where I will show you how to do 60 second videos a **different way.**

Next, we'll cover how prolific content sets the stage for you to build Pipeline Equity.

PIPELINE EQUITY - This fancy term simply means that you want to put out more goodwill content than sales content.

This is a concept I got from working in TV all of those years. 75% of the content is TV shows, news programs and weather reports that gave value to the audience, but in order to keep the TV station on air, we had to run commercials. Commercials only took up 25% of airtime, but they make TV stations very profitable.

I'm all about simplicity and if it works for TV, it works for social media too.

This is why I like a content split of 75% goodwill content and only 25% sales content.

MY IDEAL DOSE OF PIPELINE EQUITY

GOOD WILL CONTENT

SALES CONTENT

Meaning, I'm educating, giving, and inspiring a vast majority of the time, and only pitching on occasion. You'll find that you gain significant momentum with this rhythm.

Think of it this way -- each time you post value-based content, your goodwill rating with your audience goes up. You can imagine a little meter diagram filling up.

And then each time you post sales content, that goodwill meter goes down a little bit. It doesn't mean you shouldn't sell, it just means that you have to balance the selling with pure giving through value-based content.

Think about the ads that you see in your newsfeed right now. Most of the people are running the same sales ad over and over again. Their meter looks more like the image below.

THE PIPELINE EQVITY OF MOST RUNNING ADS

GOODWILL CONTENT ◢

SALES CONTENT ▨▨▨▨▨▨▨▨▨

That black spot by the goodwill content is not a smudge my friends. That is how **LITTLE** most people running ads are putting out goodwill content.

They are just hitting their audience over the head with the same sales ad over and over again.

See the opportunity?

When we get into the actual mechanics of how to put these principles into play, you'll see how the tactics I'm going to give you tie all these things together into a beautiful system.

In your opinion, who would make a better, more qualified lead for your business? Someone who randomly clicked on an ad and filled out a form for a lead magnet? Or someone who has been consistently consuming your content and feels connected to you?

There really is no wrong answer here, but for me personally, I'd rather build a ton of Pipeline Equity with a list of Invisible Leads who have been consuming my content. That way, I know they are already warm and preconditioned before they buy anything.

THE INVISIBLE LEAD - When I say an *"invisible"* lead, that means you literally cannot see the people who are on that list. This is the list that is created *on platform* by people who engage with your content.

By contrast, most gurus who emphasize conversion campaigns built their lists with *off platform* data that was tracked with a pixel.

For my newer folks, a *"pixel"* is simply a small line of code that can track off platform actions. Meaning, if you're running ads on a platform like Facebook, the pixel can still track certain actions you take when you are acting outside of Facebook. So for example, if the ad takes you to a website off of Facebook, the Facebook pixel can track that action.

If this all sounds like a foreign language to you, that's okay, because you actually don't need a pixel when you use this strategy.

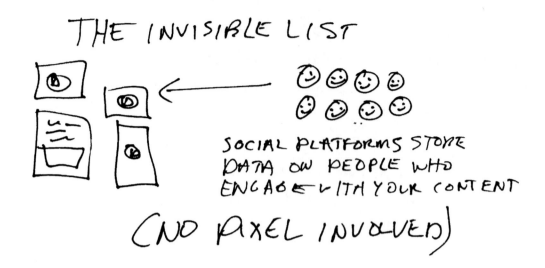

THE INVISIBLE LIST

SOCIAL PLATFORMS STORE DATA ON PEOPLE WHO ENGAGE WITH YOUR CONTENT

(NO PIXEL INVOLVED)

Even though the list is "invisible," that's okay, because while you can't see personal user info, you know that the list is made up of people who are actively consuming your content!

Make sense?

Let me tell you a story how building an invisible list literally saved my agency clients data when a "pixel fallout" happened with a new release from apple a few years ago, that allowed people to opt out of getting tracked via the pixel.

I had a client who had spent tens of thousands of dollars on ads that ran to a webinar funnel. Before the "pixel fallout" she was able to retarget people who visited her funnel and show them more ads.

When the "pixel fallout" happened, a lot of people **LOST** tracking data and essentially had to start over with building their audiences… but not my client!

Alongside of her webinar ads, I had also been running video ads to her audience who were engaging with her webinar funnel. So, even though her pixel data was lost, her warm audience was not lost. The data of those who watched videos on platform stayed **ON** the platform!

We were able to continue to run ads to her warm audience and business went on as usual. Unfortunately, that "pixel fallout" caused a lot of businesses to go under for awhile.

This is why it's important we don't just have a one dimensional strategy to bring in clients. It mitigates risk.

STEALTH CONVERSATIONS - This is one of my favorite pieces of the whole approach because it allows you to have casual conversations with people and still pitch your offer, but without actually pitching up front.

In chapter 2 I mentioned that I discovered how giving something away like a checklist or a cheat sheet brought in more comments. I also mentioned that conversations are the fastest path to cash.

So… Here we go.

The "stealthiness" of this strategy comes into play as you will offer helpful freebies, that I now call *"value bombs,"* to your prospects and use them as a way to open conversations that lead to sales.

Instead of a pure sales post, you'll be putting out videos in the newsfeed that lead to sales conversations without the burden of diminishing your goodwill in the process.

Meaning, higher Pipeline Equity because your sales posts are stealth.

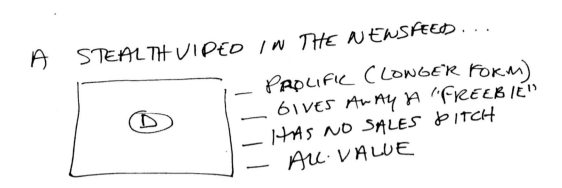

A STEALTH VIDEO IN THE NEWSFEED...

- PROLIFIC (LONGER FORM)
- GIVES AWAY A "FREEBIE"
- HAS NO SALES PITCH
- ALL VALUE

We'll dig more into this stealth content throughout the book, but for now just be aware that flying in stealth mode actually gets you better results than the more direct approach that most gurus are teaching. And it keeps your goodwill meter much higher over time.

If you focus on the nuances of this approach, you'll be in a strong position to steer your business any way you choose.

Quick recap -- the nuances of this super duper profitable ad strategy.

1. **PROLIFIC CONTENT** - Publishing long-form content that address natural human buying behavior.

2. **PIPELINE EQUITY** - Maintaining goodwill with our audience by emphasizing value based content over sales content.

3. **THE INVISIBLE LEAD** - using *on platform* retargeting based on video views campaigns.

4. **STEALTH CONVERSATIONS** - This allows us to still pitch without using typical sales ads so we can maintain Pipeline Equity.

Before we move on, I need to ask you a very important question -- If I could put you into a messenger conversation with 100 of your ideal clients, how many of those people would you be able to sell your program or service to?

Think about that for a moment.

Most people tend to think that all they need are *"more leads."* But what good does more leads do for you if they are unqualified? Or worse yet, they are qualified but don't buy because they don't really know or trust you yet.

As you progress through this book and get deeper into Content, Consistency, and Conversations, you'll realize that navigating the conversation piece is what actually puts money in the bank.

How you navigate the development of your stealth content and use of my pipeline equity framework will be the critical variables that determine how warm and pre-sold your leads are. And believe me, having conversations with pre-sold and very warm leads is way more fun (and profitable) than the teeth-pulling method that most funnel strategies create for you.

Now that you have a better understanding of why this approach works so well, let's get into all the juicy bits of the anatomy of these stealth content videos.

CHAPTER 4
THE 7-FIGURE $5 AD

Give me the next 15 minutes and I am going to walk you through the anatomy of the $5 video ad that took my business to 7 figures.

This is where the real work is about to begin!

Remember the core principles at play here. They are what makes this strategy so damn good...

1. Content
2. Consistency
3. Conversations

In this chapter, you'll get the formula that produces magnetic **Content**. And when you publish with **Consistency**, you will inevitably end up with qualified **Conversations.**

Sounds easy, right?

Not so fast there big dawg. If you don't nail the foundations, which is the structure, messaging, and video anatomy, then publishing consistently will be a waste of time! And you certainly won't produce qualified conversations, which means "no soup for you!"

Let's start with the structure.

Below is a diagram of what a stealth video looks like in your newsfeed. I call these stealth videos, **Power Content.**

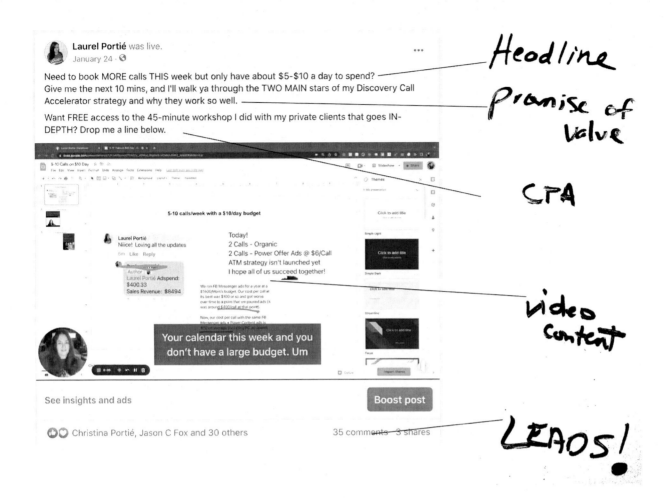

Notice, I am using video content to draw in my ideal client and then offering them a value bomb that they can "raise their hand" by commenting to get. They are initially inviting me to have a conversation with them.

Now that you can visually see the principles at work, you're probably asking yourself, what the heck goes **INTO** the actual video script.

I'll get to that.

But before I tell you the anatomy to this very profitable $5 video ad, I have to tell you how I came up with my Power Content concept and why this works so well.

Remember when I told you about my days as a television producer?

I have worked for CBS, FOX and various syndication companies, but it was where I started my very first job that handed me this amazing secret that I'm about to share with you.

Back in 2002, even before I started experimenting with social media channels, I had one of the hardest jobs ever…Getting people to watch the 11 o'clock news.

When I say the 11 o'clock news… I am talking about the 11PM "sleepy time snoozefest" news that aired after their favorite prime time television show.

My job was to write a 30 second commercial that promoted what was coming up on the 11pm newscast.

As soon as those credits rolled… I had to do two things **VERY WELL** if I wanted to keep my job.

1. I needed to grab viewers' attention **BEFORE** they grabbed the remote
2. I had to **KEEP** their attention through a 3-minute commercial break

There are a lot of things working against me at that point. It's 11-freaking PM. Many people are fighting sleep or they're fighting the urge to have S-E-X with their partner (let's be **REAL**)!

As a matter of fact, it became a running joke in our nightly pitch meetings that my news director would say…

"Laurel, we need a promo so sexy, that it will "keep honey waiting."

(Eventually you'll be so good at this process that your ads will be sexy enough to "keep honey waiting.")

I'll give you an example of what it looked like for me back in 2008.

Everyone loved the hit TV show CSI Miami…well at least they did back in the day. So let's imagine that it's come to a heart-stopping ending to CSI Miami and the credits start rolling.

This is my cue to do those two things:

1. I have to grab my audience's attention

2. I have to keep it…through this 3-minute commercial break.

But, here's something that's also super important to be aware of. Not **ALL** news is relevant to **ALL** viewers. How can I make a story that's only impacting one neighborhood relevant to our entire viewing audience?

I'll give you a real example of one of the **BIGGEST** challenges I had on a **SLOW** news night.

A water main break on the side of interstate 20 right outside of Dallas, TX.

How the heck do I make **THAT** sexy?

Challenge accepted.

Here's what I wrote.

CUE credits for CSI Miami

"**WAIT!** Before you hit the sack… In the next 5 minutes, find out why TEXDOT says you'll want to set your alarm clock an hour early or you might be late for work tomorrow. Full story next at 11.

Do ya see what I did there?

The story was actually about a water main break. How freaking boring is a water main break?!

But, I had to figure out a way to make this water main break *relevant* to the people who are watching my TV station.

If I would have just simply said… "Next at 11, take a look at this water main break and look at what authorities are doing to clean it up."

(This is likely the style many of you are writing your ads right now!)

That definitely would not have gotten people to stay and watch the 11 o'clock news. **WHO CARES** about spraying water unless you live in that neighborhood?

I had to dig deeper.

I had to think… ***How could this possibly have an effect on my audience if they don't get this fixed tonight?***

(and by the way, you'll want to underline that paragraph above and tuck it away in the back of your brain so you can use it later… because when you know what happens to your audience if they don't fix their problems, and you are able to call it out clearly and effectively, you will reap the rewards both in authority and financial gain.)

I realized, if they don't get this fixed tonight… Two lanes of this major highway will be closed and there's going to be a huge pile up of traffic tomorrow morning.

That is going to affect a lot of people!

Also take note, I added in the element of time. I told them in the next 5 minutes, they will know the answer.

After hearing my promo, a lot of my viewers probably thought it was worth the 5 minutes of their time to stay up and watch the 11pm News to see **WHY** they should set their alarm clocks a little earlier tomorrow.

That's super relevant to them because if they're late for work… they're going to get in trouble and could possibly lose an hour or two of pay. That's **IMPORTANT** to them.

That is the promise of VALUE.

(again, underline that one. Until you can clearly communicate a promise of value, it's unlikely that your target market will respond to your messaging).

That is what I had to figure out every single night.

So, what I'm about to teach you is going to follow that same concept. You need to figure out what value you can give to your audience and *why* it's worth their time to watch your video.

So without further delay, here it is! The anatomy of the $5 "Power Content" ad that took my business to 7 figures.

ANATOMY OF THE $5 POWER CONTENT AD

The anatomy of the $5 Power Content ad is made up of 5 parts:

Part 1: The Headline

Part 2: The Promise of Value

Part 3: The CTA ("call to action" for my newcomers)

Part 4: The Humble Brag

Part 5: The Content

We want to look at the flow of these parts… as a funnel.

The first line's **ONLY** job is to get people to say, "This is for me and I **NEED** to read the second line."

(hehe, now you'll look at every headline you see with this filter… and it will drive you nuts! But it will also be super educational)

The second line's **ONLY** job is to get people to **WATCH** our video.

The Video's **ONLY** job is to get people to take action.

But if we can't get people past the first line, what's the point?

Pause for just one moment, and revisit that one.

If we can't get people past the first line, what's the point?!

If you truly believe in the service or program you are offering the world, and you know that it can genuinely help people, then you owe it to them to put in that extra effort to craft your message so that they can finally see and understand how you'll help them.

THAT is where most online marketers go wrong. They are not following this ***"Funnel Flow"*** for their video content.

They are not looking at their video as a funnel in and of itself. They are just treating the entire thing as one piece of content.

But now that you know better, you have the power!

Each individual line is its own piece of content, getting viewers to the next step. Ready to dig in and try it out?

Take a look at that diagram again. This is the **ANATOMY** of what the video ad will actually look like.

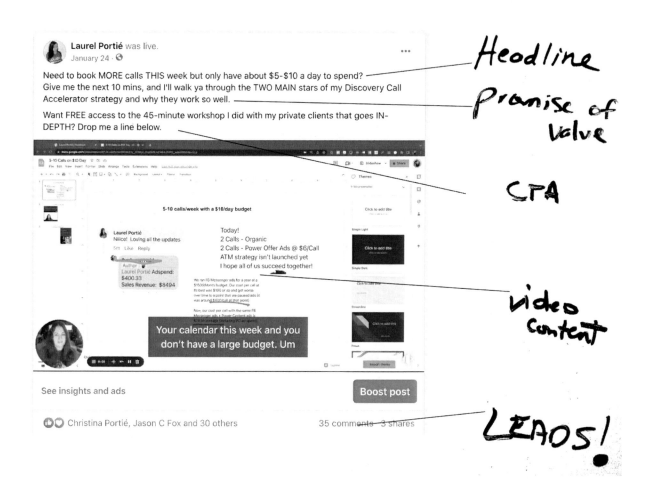

THE PROMISE OF VALUE

Here's a little trick I use to create the most compelling copy. Even though part 1 is the headline, I actually write the promise of value first as I prepare the ad.

When you do it this way, the headline becomes much juicier and more compelling.

Anytime I see my students struggle with this script, I tell them to start with the promise of value, and it works like a charm.

It literally rewires your brain to think from your client's perspective rather than thinking primarily of an exciting tag line.

Remember my example above: I first considered how the water main break might hurt my audience before I considered how to communicate with them about how to avoid that pain.

In other words - *empathy*.

Your ability to operate and create from a foundation of empathy for those you serve will literally make or break your business.

So take a deep breath, and let's get empathetic...

What is the **ONE** promise you can make to your audience, that if they watch this video, they will get _____ out of it?

If you go back to the beginning of this chapter, you can see I used this super cool script to get you to read it.

"Give me the next 15 minutes and I am going to walk you through the anatomy of the $5 video ad that took my business to 7 figures."

It made ya read it, didn't it? I like putting a time frame in there because it builds trust. You know that this will only be 15 minutes of your time invested **AND** I promised you'd be able to launch your own $5 ad after reading this chapter.

So now that we have a promise of value. We will go back to the first line, which is the headline.

THE HEADLINE

This **HAS** to grab people's attention.

Remember, the **ONLY** job of the headline is to get people to say "This is me, I want to learn more"

But… The headline also has to be **SUPER** repelling.

We do not want anyone who is not our ideal customer watching this video. Do not be afraid to be polarizing.

For instance, in this book, I want to repel people who have no intention of doing video marketing.

Scroll back up and look at my headline. See what I did there? I was **CLEAR** on what type of strategy you were going to read about.

I was polarizing to all the business owners who do not want to use video.

Now take a look at the diagram I posted above. The Headline is "Need to book MORE calls THIS week but only have about $5 to $10 a day to spend?"

I'm grabbing attention with a compelling statement that solves an immediate need and creates urgency. Then, I'm polarizing with the piece about only having a $5 to $10 budget.

THE CALL TO ACTION

You're probably wondering why I put a call to action so high in the video.

The main reason is for early engagement. The sooner we can get people to comment below the video, the faster Facebook and YouTube will deliver it to more people in the newsfeed.

But what's more important, is that this *"Value Bomb"* strategy gets you **CONVERSATIONS** with leads who are your ideal clients. Conversations are the fastest path to cash.

Again, review that example. See what I'm doing?

If someone wants free access to the 45-minute workshop that delivers the promise of value, they have to comment on that post. Every comment is a new lead to open up a conversation with.

THE HUMBLE BRAG

A lot of business owners fail to do this in any of their videos but these 3-4 lines will make you **HIGHLY** referable. I'll give you an example so you can see what I mean.

Following the CTA in my videos, I always say the same 3-4 lines.

"My name is Laurel Portie. I'm the owner of adcoachingfor7.com where I have now taught over 10,000 coaches and consultants how to launch and optimize their own online ads. In every single video, you're going to get one advertising strategy you can immediately implement after watching."

I have several tactics going on there and by repeating these lines in **ALL** my videos, my audience will...

1. Know my name
2. Know my website
3. Know what I do and how I can help them
4. Know that in EVERY video they will get one thing they can implement.

This makes me not only highly referable, but anytime people see a new video of mine, they have a compelling reason to watch! They will be scared to miss that important nugget they can implement. ;)

THE CONTENT

The #1 reason most people don't buy a product or service is because they don't have clarity on what they will actually get if they work with you or buy your product.

And the only reason they don't have that clarity is because... you guessed it, the messaging lacks empathy!

So many experts are teaching their students to only reveal the "what", but to never reveal the "how." I do not agree with this. My thought is that if I can give people absolute clarity on what I can/will do for them, it will be a no-brainer for them to want to work with me.

On that note, if you watch examples of my content across my YouTube channel, www.*youtube.com/thelaurelshow*, you will see that my content gives away the farm. I reveal my exact ad strategies, my ad setups, my content secrets, my copy tactics and **EVERYTHING** I teach my students in my programs.

Heck, I'm even giving you the actual strategy in this book and then inviting you to get more on the YouTube Channel!

Why?

When people decide they want to work with me, I don't have to spend hours and hours teaching things that are highly mundane to me. I want to spend time **personalizing** the strategies and tactics.

My free content is literally "creating" my ideal client.

I'm not saying this is what **you** need to do, but this way of thinking has served me and my private clients well.

So the question becomes -- how can you showcase your skills to your audience?

What can you show them that will make them say…

"I need to work with this person!"

"Wow, I didn't know how to do that, I want to learn more from this person!"

"I want them to do **THAT** for me!"

Most of my agency clients hired me on the spot because my content gave them *clarity* that I was not a fake guru. My free content allowed them to watch me launch ad strategies, write copy and even build out funnel structures on the fly.

In other words, I just pulled back the curtain and showed them what it's like to work together.

I know you'll be tempted to dangle the carrot and withhold information because you think you're "giving away the farm."

But the reality is, people are not paying for your info, they're paying you to help them get where they want to go *faster* and with less resistance.

Now that you have a firm foundation on how this stuff works, watch my WORKSHOP on creating Power Content For Your Business:

www.adswithlaurel.com/powercontent

CHAPTER 5
CREATING CONVERSATION CASH

"Conversations are the fastest path to cash."

Now, before we go deeper into this next part of the process, we need to pause for just a moment and review two critical factors that will determine how effective this chapter will be for you.

1. The content creation strategy only works if you understand your own process or methodology on a deep level.

2. You have to be able to diagnose the smallest micro-step your prospect can take within 10 minutes in order to get a small win.

If you're struggling with one or both of these elements, you might want to hop into the group with thousands of other coaches and service providers to get some personalized help and support from me and the community.

You can view those details here:
https://www.adcoachingfor7.com/

But once those two pieces are squared away, you can start generating conversations and cash, which is exactly what the Conversion Multiplier strategy is built to do.

Everyone always asks me... "Laurel, where do those 60 second reels videos fit into your strategy?"

Well, here is where they fit.

First we have to understand that our Power Content videos are prolific. They have a purpose of goodwill and building a list of invisible leads. The *bonus* is, because of the value bomb element, they can lead to quick conversations.

THE PURPOSE OF POWER CONTENT

- BUILDS PIPELINE EQUITY (GOODWILL WITH YOUR AUDIENCE)
- BUILDS INVISIBLE LIST (PEOPLE WHO WATCH 25% OR MORE)
- CAN START CONVERSATIONS VIA THE VALUE BOMB (THE FREE THING YOU'RE GIVING AWAY)

But building authority with your ideal customer relies on more than just creating video content. We have to create content that is going to help us connect with them on a deeper level.

We have to create content that is going to allow them to tell us what type of information they need from us in order to help them solve their problems.

Remember, **building authority requires connection.**

Connection begins with empathy and is strengthened by the relevant video content you create.

Many internet marketers will tell you that you should be producing dozens of pieces of content a week. But there are only so many hours in the week, and the most successful entrepreneurs I know are the ones who understand how to maximize efficiency so they don't grind themselves into the ground.

Most of you guys who are reading this right now need clients, right?

Producing dozens of pieces of content a week is a strategy built for impressions, or in other words, eyeballs. Most of you guys do not need more impressions, you need **CLIENTS**. The recurring theme throughout this book has been that conversations are the fastest path to cash.

Ironically, the main guru that people are copying for short form video content says in all of his content…

"I have nothing to sell you."

We, on the other hand, need to sell in order to grow our business, so we will use short form in a slightly different way.

This strategy I am about to outline for you is built to get 100 new messenger conversations a week.

Why 100?

I know, 100 is an arbitrary number, but it ensures that we get the volume **EVERY WEEK** in order to identify the following 2 types of prospects.

1. Who are your 10 hottest prospects
2. Who are your 10 warmest prospects

While most of the online space is copying major influencers who are using short form videos as a way to get impressions, we will use them to get warm and hot prospects into our messenger.

Pause here. Don't gloss over that last sentence. We will be using short form video to create **warm** and **hot** prospects. If you publish video just for the sake of impressions, you will be collecting eyeballs and followers, which is not the same as building an audience of people who will buy from you.

Each week you'll only need to create 1-3 of the following short form content.

Right now, Instagram Reels are the "thing" but you can execute this across any platform that allows short form video.

Each video is designed to start conversations. These posts won't necessarily get you a sale today, but by opening up conversations with people who need your help, you'll be able to gently guide your prospects to that moment of enrollment.

Let's take a closer look at each one of these shorts and how to craft them.

One important element you'll need is something you've already created when you did your Power Content and that is a value bomb. We are essentially going to create a 60 second video that solely promotes your value bomb.

This will **ACCELERATE** the process at which we will get conversations.

With our Power Content videos, we led with value. Whereas this part of the strategy just straight up offers to give them that value bomb (or bribe) in order to have a conversation.

I want to say this again, we do NOT want to ask them for an email or send them to ANY type of optin.

I know, that's the opposite of every other program out there, lol! But the sooner you stop drinking guru-juice, the sooner you can get some real momentum!

We want to simply give them the value bomb in messenger. I'll get to my messenger framework here in a minute, right now I just want you to understand the strategy and the type of video to do.

The strategy looks like this:

60 SECOND VIDEO → COMMENT → MESSENGER

So, what do you say in that video? I will give you *THREE* of my best scripts.

SCRIPT OPTION #1

How to [Result] in [Timeframe] Without [Thing You Hate Doing]

Hey [Target Audience]

Here's why [what are they currently doing isn't working]

[Tell them why what they are currently doing isn't working]

[Tell them what you're doing– and why it works]

I've put together a guide that [gets the result they're looking for]

Before now… I've ONLY shared with my private clients.

But I'd like to give it to you just for watching this video.

Drop me a line below this video if you want it.

SCRIPT OPTION #2

Hey [Target Audience]

This checklist has the [Name of Value Bomb] and I want to give it to you, absolutely free…

People like [Name of Client] used it just last week to go from [Where they were to where they are now]

(Insert social proof screenshot)

I also put this into the hands of [Name of another client] that went from [Where they were to where they are now]

(Insert social proof screenshot)

Drop me a line below this video and I'll put it in your hands so you can [Get desired result], deal?

SCRIPT OPTION #3

Hey [Target Audience]

[Identify A Problem]

Here's why [what are they currently doing isn't working]

I just did a training with my private clients that showed them how to [Solve That Problem] using [Your Unique Mechanism]

If you'd like to see a replay of that training…

Drop me a line below this video with a [Code word] and I'll send it to your messenger–

I won't even ask for your email address!

My gift for watching this video.

This will generate a **TON** of comments, especially if you take the video and place it as a $5 ad in the ads manager.

Here's what *every* conversation multiplier post looks like when I post it on Instagram

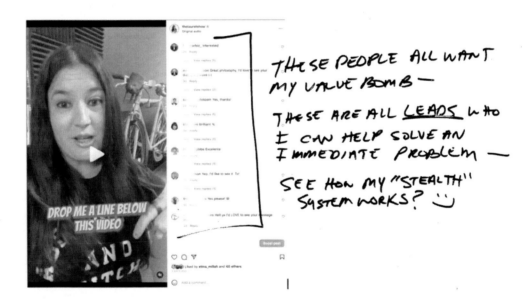

I used one of the scripts above, and promoted my value bomb. I told my audience to "Drop me a line below this video" if they wanted it.

You can see, the comments started flying in.

That's the easy part…

How do you turn those comments into **clients?**

I'm glad you asked.

First of all, I approach the conversation as if that person has just paid me $500 to help them solve their most urgent and immediate challenge in the next 10 minutes.

Sounds simple enough, right? But that one mental shift will forever change how you approach these conversations. Because it's no longer a messenger spam fest where you apply external pressure to get them to do what you want them to do.

Instead, it's now an **actually** helpful interaction that moves them forward (gasp! Imagine that!)

This is absolutely critical because way too often I see that my students are trying to solve **too much** for the client all at once.

You only have a few minutes with this prospect in messenger, so you want to solve the most immediate concern.

For example, if someone wants to scale from $5k/month to $30k/month, I'm not going to be able to give them everything they need in 10 minutes.

Instead, I would first have to ask them a series of diagnostic questions to figure out what their most immediate next step **should** be. That way I can give them relevant counsel based on where they're at.

In my case, I might ask something like, "okay, what have you already been doing that got you to $5k/month?"

And let's say they've been doing organic Instagram posts that sell their program but they only have around 2,000 followers.

The *easiest* micro-step that I could help them take in 10 minutes is showing them how to place a $5 ad on the posts that are already attracting clients. This will drive more volume so they could do their thing.

Most gurus would tell them to do something silly…

"Just build a webinar funnel bro"

That's not a micro-step, that's a huge step that will likely drive that person into a profit deficit and take weeks if not months, to actually get results.

I'll give you an example.

One of my newest private clients in my Lean on Laurel program (this is my inner circle type program)... Came to me after spending over 22K in adspend on a webinar funnel that resulted in **ZERO** booked appointments.

He was getting a *TON* of leads, meaning people were opting into his funnel and watching his webinar, but they weren't moving on to book a call.

The coach he was working with kept telling him he needed to change his offer.

Within 5 minutes of diving into his metrics, the problem wasn't his offer. People weren't even getting to his offer.

His numbers showed that 34% of people gave him their name and email address in exchange for watching the webinar. That's pretty good, **BUT** the problem was that only 9% of those people who had opted in were actually hitting play on the webinar and a mere .02% had actually made it to the offer.

What does that mean?

His offer wasn't the problem, at least not yet.

Immediately seeing this "black hole" in his funnel, I had him break down his webinar into 1 "easy-to-digest" value bomb.

I then quickly wrote 3 "short" scripts using the SAME templates I just walked you through that promoted that value bomb.

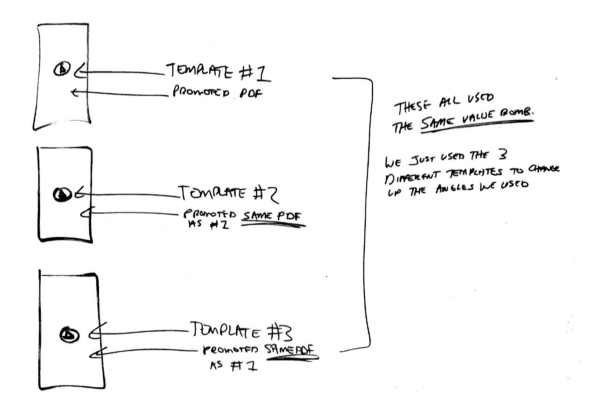

I launched those short videos inside his ads manager for $5 a day and the messages started flooding in.

Long story short, he had over 170 messenger conversations in one weekend and booked over 65 calls, for less than $100 in adspend.

So let's recap.

- He spent $22K on a webinar funnel that yielded **ZERO** booked calls.

- I helped him launch this "conversion multiplier" short video strategy and he booked 65 calls with less than $100.

I have sooooo many stories just like that one.

So many people are putting too many steps in front of having a conversation with a prospect.

What I am walking you through in this chapter fixes that.

Now, to the goods…

How to handle diagnostics in messenger. This will sound way too simple to work, but I promise, if you put this into practice, you will see results pretty quickly.

If you're wondering what those diagnostic questions should be, here's a fun little thought exercise that can help:

1. Write down the top 3 problems that your client faces.

2. Under each problem, write out 5 questions that will help you understand the *details* of that problem.

Now, this is not the be-all end-all of diagnostic assessment. It's just a way to get started if you're struggling with what to ask specifically.

Quick example: let's say you have a nutrition coaching offer, and one of your prospect's main problems is that they have intense cravings in the middle of the afternoon, and those cravings push them to eat overly fatty, sugary, and salty snacks in the middle of their day. This of course leads to an energy crash later in the day, and weight gain long term.

In order to diagnose what's really going on before sending that prospect a value bomb, you might ask "what do you eat for breakfast?" or "what supplements are you currently taking?" or "when was the last time you had bloodwork taken to measure hormone levels?" or "what are your sleep patterns like?"

Remember the frame -- I'm trying to help them take *just* the next most immediate step forward in the next 10 minutes. And those cravings could be coming from many different sources, so I want to diagnose what the most likely source is.

Now you can take this principle and apply it directly to your context, regardless of which niche or audience you serve.

To recap -- every single week you will only need to create 1-2 of these videos with the value bomb offer.

But wait, there's more…

Once you have 3 videos that hit with your audience, you *don't* have to create more. You would just continue running those 3 videos as ads and the comments and conversations will continue to come pouring in.

You've now proven that specific organic content works and that it resonates with your audience, so now you can put some dollars behind it.

AUTOMATED BABY!

Now the ads manager is doing all the heavy lifting and all you need to do is keep an eye on comments and respond to those comments in your messenger.

In the next chapter I am going to show you a $500/month ad strategy that uses Power Content and Conversion Multipliers to consistently book 5-10 discovery calls for my clients each week.

You're about to see how the $5 ads will pull in your ideal audience and then I'll show you how $2 ads will consistently nurture that audience until they buy.

But before you move on, be sure to view this short video about the messenger framework:

www.adswithlaurel.com/messenger

CHAPTER 6

PUTTING THE FUN IN FUNNELS

Alright, now the real fun can begin!

You didn't think that I was just going to let you read this book and do nothing, did ya?

In this chapter, I am going to give you a play-by-play on getting this *entire* system up over the next 7 days. **NO EXCUSES.**

If you can do each item over the next 7 days, you will be worlds ahead of most of your competitors and you **WILL** win new clients.

Remember my client Scott I mentioned in chapter 2? This is what he uses.

It's what my clients put into play to reduce their cost per booked call by 90%!

It's what my private clients use to book calls with prospective clients for less than $20!

$10K Month!!

$754 Adspend

(With all those page issues, relaunching ads every few days from a new page)

I calculate every 20th of the month (we still have a few days to go).

OO 3   2 comments

Booked 3 calls from ads today @ $11/Call!

$401 Adspend
$8.5K Sales

And of course, this is the process I used when I told you earlier that I hit the $1M mark with only $36,000 in ad spend.

In chatting with over 10,000 students over the years, I've learned that on average people are spending 4-6 hours per day on social media trying to promote their business! And let's be honest, a lot of that is probably scrolling and browsing, not real productive action.

They think that more is better, but the reality is that most of those hours are simply wasted. Instead of actual money-generating activities, it usually just becomes aimless wandering.

Can you relate? Do you often find yourself feeling stuck inside social media, but not getting the traction that you see others getting?

Thing is, I'm willing to admit that if I didn't give myself, or my clients, a daily checklist, we would end up wasting hours every day on social media, just browsing around and scrolling.

I hope you guys are ready to rock n roll, and I mean **today** not tomorrow.

This is where the work begins.

I'll tell you guys something I tell my students all the time, and excuse my language…

"F* TOMORROW!"**

Right now, I'm giving you the opportunity to get ahead of 90% of your competitors, but only you can set the tone of how **fast** you will move.

If you wait until tomorrow, there's already someone doing it today. That compounds over time.

Think about this.

I started my digital business at the **same time** as a lot of really awesome people – I didn't waste time. I got my videos out there – I got on free strategy calls for 100 days straight.

I don't have more hours in the day than everyone else– but I got my data out there faster so I could see the **gaps** I was missing in my content. Then I fixed them and my progress kept compounding and compounding.

For those of you who are a little apprehensive about doing ads, I tell my students all of the time… "Ads are just organic content with money on it."

If you implement what I teach in this chapter, after 90 days you will have the data you need to fix what's not optimized. Problem is, most people aren't that patient.

I know for a fact that 75% of the people who will read this playbook will do nothing with it. And that's okay.

The only difference between success and staying where you are— is the speed at which you execute after making a decision.

I want to be transparent here -- 9 out of 10 ads I will place will fail. I did a lot of failing to get a handful of winners that took my business to 7-figures.

The first step to success is what I'll call **"Task Zero."** It's like a pre-checklist item. It's when you finally acknowledge that more hours doesn't necessarily equal higher productivity. Time spent in social media isn't necessarily directly related to generating more money for your business.

However, when you have the right list of high output actions, then you don't need to spend 4-6 hours each day spinning your wheels.

Here's a diagram of what you'll be implementing over the next 7 days.

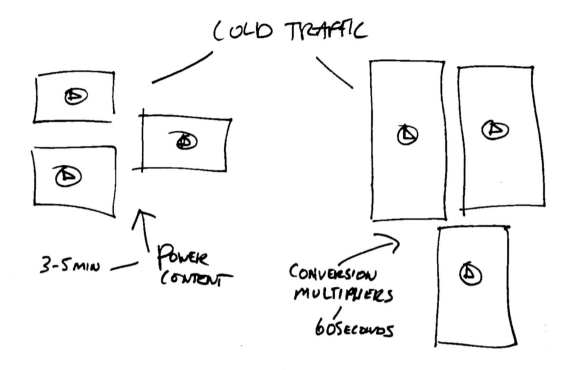

Take note, we will only be focusing on content for cold traffic this week. We cannot run retargeting ads if we do not have enough people who have watched our cold traffic content.

Don't worry, we will break each of the assignments down by day with all of the fun details on execution.

Before we get started creating the videos, we have to remember **why** we are doing these videos. We're doing these videos in order to **hook** our ideal clients. Once we get them to watch a certain % of this first set of videos, they will start to get our other content.

Think about this, if we want our ideal clients to watch these videos, then we have to insert another element to keep our **not** ideal clients out. The best way to do that is by using polarizing content.

I'll tell you a short story about how I messed this up in the beginning.

While I was at a mastermind with my mentor, Nic, I approached him with a very serious concern. *"Everyone who's applying for my advanced program seems to be a beginner! Why is that happening?"*

He took one look at my content and had me change a **single** word.

He said, *"Stop telling people you'll help them launch their ads."* *Tell them you'll help them **"fix"** their ads, instead."*

A lightbulb immediately went off and I never had that problem again.

We want to protect our retargeting ecosystem. We want to make sure we are attracting **only** our ideal clients with our power content otherwise we will end up spending money retargeting people who are not our ideal clients.

Before you jump into the daily actions below, I highly recommend you view this workshop I did recently. It will give the overview of the funnel and some explanation. Then, I'll walk you through the details in the remainder of this chapter.

<u>www.adswithlaurel.com/500</u>

The video will give you some context for what we cover in this chapter and it will help you absorb and retain more of the strategy in preparation for when you implement it.

Very few of my students grasp the full scope of this strategy on their first time through it, and that's okay! As long as you're willing to study this material consistently, you will become an ads champion, and your bank account will reflect that.

Okay, so *now* let's get to work.

THE 7-DAY ACTION PLAN

- ☐ **Day 1** - Create your first value bomb and determine your topics for your 3 power content and conversion multiplier videos

- ☐ **Day 2** - Write and launch Power content video #1

- ☐ **Day 3** - Write and launch Power content video #2

- ☐ **Day 4** - Write and launch Power content video #3

- ☐ **Day 5** - Write and launch Conversion Multiplier #1

- ☐ **Day 6** - Write and launch Conversion Multiplier #2

- ☐ **Day 7** - Write and launch Conversion Multiplier #3

PRO TIPS FOR CREATING A GREAT VALUE BOMB

Just to refresh your memory, a value bomb will be the conversation starter for both your Power Content and your conversion multiplier. It's the freebie you're giving to your audience for watching the video but it's also the gateway to having a sales conversation.

Don't overthink it. Most of my value bombs are simple google documents. It's not about how pretty it is, but about solving your prospect's most immediate problem and then highlighting the next problem that needs to be solved.

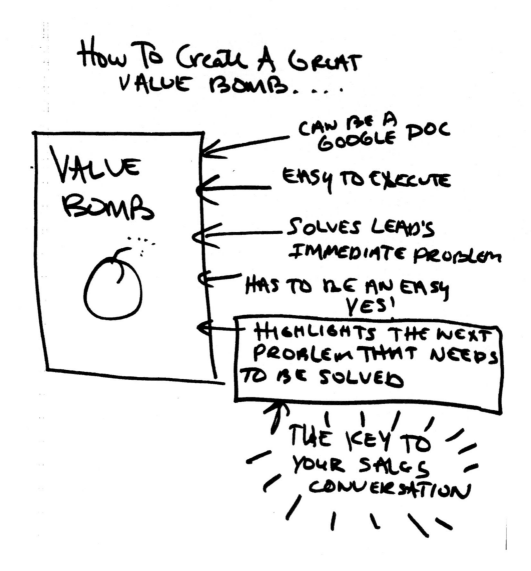

The main reason why a lot of value bombs don't work is because they just help someone solve a problem. They don't highlight the next problem that needs to be solved.

I'll give you an example.

One of my best value bombs is my Conversion Multiplier reels strategy that I'm teaching you guys here in this book.

Every week I get over 200 people asking for that value bomb and over 40 people come back to me saying…

"Laurel! That worked so well, but I'm struggling with turning those comments into messenger conversations that sell my product."

That sounds like a bigger problem I can help them solve, right?

It's a no-brainer for those who can afford my personalized coaching to apply for my Lean on Laurel program and for those who can't to join my $7 program where they can get my help on doing that.

This is where a lot of consultants miss the mark and their leads never move into the sales process. They just stay in free content land forever.

POWER CONTENT FOR COLD TRAFFIC

Over the next 3 days we will write, record and launch your first pieces of power content in the ads manager. I've got my little notebook out and I am working through this funnel **with** you as I am writing this book.

Take note, these videos will be going to **cold** traffic.

There will be **TWO** places where we will need copy.

1. The actual video itself

2. The copy for the video ad

You'll notice that the ad copy is *super* short. It will only contain the first 3 lines of the overall video copy.

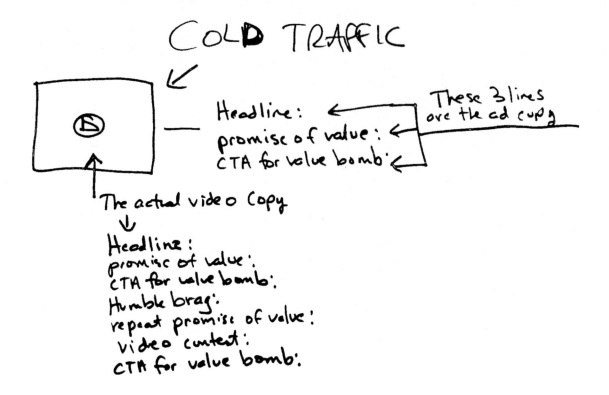

Because you likely need a little refresher on the video framework, I've written it above in the diagram for you. For those of you who can't read my chicken scratch, it's:

    1. Headline

    2. Promise of value

    3. Call to action for your value bomb

    4. Humble brag

    5. Repeat your promise of value

    6. Video content

    7. CTA for value bomb

If you've already forgotten what each of those mean, you can go back and reference chapter 4.

Anytime my students are doing this exercise with me, they often ask me...

"Laurel, I still don't know what to talk about in my video to attract my ideal clients."

Here's an easy way to get started.

Think of 3 of the most common problems you solve for your clients. Here are some of the most common video topics for some of the niches I work with.

Fitness coaches:

1. Clients are doing the wrong exercise for their goal
2. Clients are eating the wrong diet for their goal
3. Clients are using the wrong equipment for their goal

Business coaches:

1. Clients are charging too little for their services
2. Clients are using the wrong funnel to attract clients
3. Clients are not able to close clients on sales calls

Done for You Agencies:

1. Clients don't know the red flags for imposters
2. Clients don't know the KPIs for success
3. Clients are in the dark about strategies being executed

Leadership/Self Development coaches:

1. Clients are letting employees walk all over them

2. Lack of confidence when giving a presentation

3. They get passed on every promotion

Once you've figured out 3 problems your ideal clients face, it's time to write, shoot and launch videos that will directly tell them you have the solution to their problem.

Reminder: Keep these 3 videos between 3 and 5 minutes

LAUNCHING YOUR 3 POWER CONTENT VIDEOS IN ADS MANAGER

The first campaign we will launch will be our Power Content campaign. We will optimize it for *VIDEO VIEWS*.

Anxiety people have about launching their ads is centered around two things:

1. The buttons
2. Targeting

What if I told you that those two things only matter about 20% combined. The secret to successful ads has almost nothing to do with either of these things, and everything to do with the content. This is why I will not spend a lot of time on these two things.

Let's start with breaking down anxiety number one, the buttons.

Let's say that I create a power content video that says…

"This video will walk you through the process of turning any failed ad into a winning ad in just 24 hours"

I tell Facebook or YouTube to put that video in front of an audience I choose.

But oops, I run it as an engagement campaign instead of a video views campaign. Do you really think **no one** would watch that video? It would be silly to think that. Yes, certain campaigns are optimized to do more actions than others, but a good piece of content in front of the right audience will **ALWAYS** win no matter which buttons you choose.

Here's how I think about it…

Videos go **VIRAL** all the time organically. Someone sees a great piece of content and then shares it and before we know it, millions of people have seen it. There was no "optimizing" the way the video got out, it just got out.

See what I mean?

Now, onto the next anxiety… targeting.

I keep it really simple, no matter the platform. If you just spend 5 minutes inside the audience manager of **any** ads platform, you'll be able to find at least 1 audience you can run your ad to.

All of the ad platforms let you target people based on:

Interests (brands, books, tools, influencers/celebrities.. etc)
Behaviors (business owners, frequent travelers, etc)
Job Titles (real estate agent, ceo, bookkeeper, etc)
Demographics (parents, age, location.. etc)

Right now, I know what some of you are thinking… Well, I'm in the health space and I can't target anyone who's suffering from health issues.

Or, "I'm in X niche and they don't have any targeting options for me."

I want you to stop looking at targeting as one dimensional. Sure, platforms make it super easy for you to target for certain niches and impossible for others.

Just this week as I am writing this chapter I did an ads workshop and someone asked…

"I have an anxiety course, how do I target people with anxiety? The ads platform doesn't have ANY interests or tools that I can target for people with anxiety."

Before I answered her question directly, I took the audience back to the old days, when I worked in TV. We couldn't "target" specific audiences. The BEST targeting that I could do was:

- Play toy commercials during Saturday morning cartoons

- Play women's product commercials during afternoon soap operas

- Play beer commercials during sporting events

See where this is going?

For hundreds of years…whether it's been through newspaper, radio, television or billboards, tens of thousands of businesses have had successful advertising campaigns without the specific targeting options that these social platforms have given us.

So, how do I use social media to find certain audiences that can't be targeted based on certain niche problems?

We find the **PEOPLE**.

It took me less than 5 minutes to google and find out that most of the people who suffer from anxiety in the U.S. are women.

So, right there, that cuts out **HALF** of the U.S. population.

The next thing I read is that the age group that it mostly affects is 33-44 year olds.

So now we are left with only a few million women in the U.S.

We can take it even further.

The 3 industries that anxiety mostly effects are:

1. Education
2. Social Services
3. Community Services

So now, all we have to do is throw in some of those industries into the targeting and BOOM…

We are targeting based on the **PERSON**.

The ads will take care of the rest.

I'll repeat a statement I've already said in this book, but I'll say it again,

Targeting begins with your video ad content.

Your video has to attract your ideal client. It will find its way to your ideal client one way or another (just like viral videos do).

Now that we've eliminated two of the biggest anxieties people have with launching, it's time to launch these video ads in the ads platform of your choice.

My favorites at the time of writing this book…

Facebook
Instagram
YouTube

Remember, you don't need a large budget. I run each of these videos for only $5/day.

If you'd like to follow me step-by-step in setting them up, just go to:

www.adswithlaurel.com/setups

LAUNCHING YOUR CONVERSION MULTIPLIERS TO COLD TRAFFIC

Pat yourself on the back. Right now you should have your 3 Power Content videos running to a targeted audience. As we speak, it's gathering new eyeballs on your content and creating an *"invisible list"* of people watching your video.

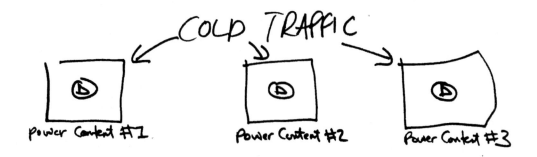

Next up, we are going to launch our conversion multipliers. These are those 60 second reels that promote your value bomb.

The goal of these conversion multiplier videos is to *start conversations*.

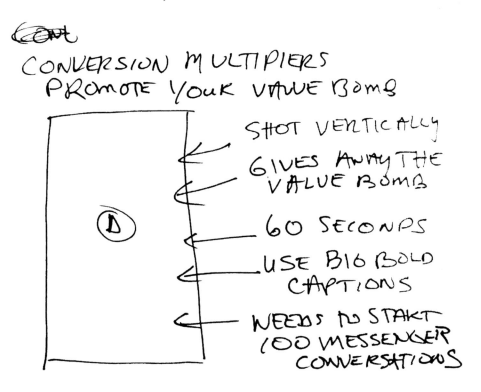

Remember, the conversion multiplier is giving away a value bomb.

The call to action is for them to comment below the video to receive that value bomb.

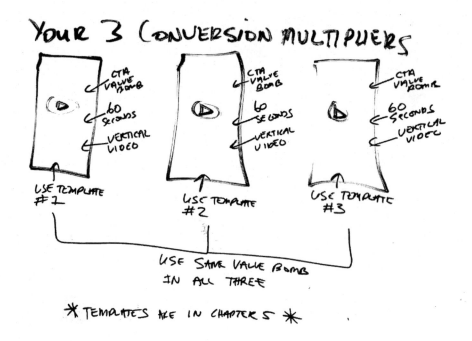

YOUR 3 CONVERSION MULTIPLIERS

USE SAME VALUE BOMB IN ALL THREE

* TEMPLATES ARE IN CHAPTER 5 *

We are going to use the **SAME** targeting we used to launch our Power Content videos.

So right now, you should have these 2 campaigns going…

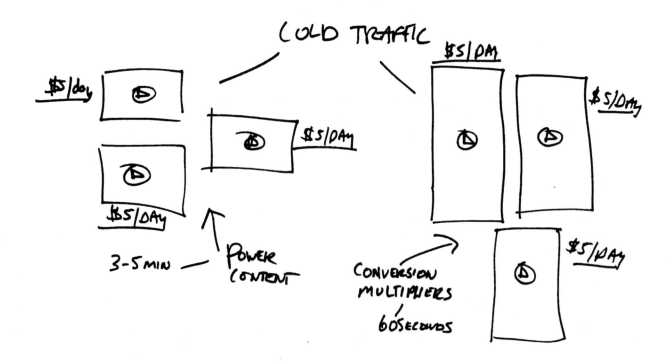

COLD TRAFFIC

Campaign 1: Optimized for Video Views

Audience | $5/day | Power Content Video 1

Audience | $5/day | Power Content Video 2

Audience | $5/day | Power Content Video 3

Campaign 2: Optimized for Engagement

Audience | $5/day | Conversion Multiplier Video 1

Audience | $5/day | Conversion Multiplier Video 2

Audience | $5/day | Conversion Multiplier Video 3

Be sure to review the workshop after you've read this chapter:

www.adswithlaurel.com/500

And when you're ready to have that feeling of flow on a regular basis, get personalized help, and jam with thousands of other entrepreneurs doing the same, just show up here:

https://www.adcoachingfor7.com/

CHAPTER 7
THE FINAL STRETCH

I know what you're thinking, because at this point in the game my students think it too….. "I'm all done, now what?"

Hold on there.

The ecosystem is *launched*, but now the **HARD** work begins.

Things are about to get real. This is where students' motivation either goes through the roof or they get frustrated and give up after the first failure.

They get discouraged when their Power Content isn't getting watched or their Conversion Multipliers aren't getting comments.

But keep in mind - the process is the shortcut!

And in this case, stumbling and "failing" is the process. As long as you know how to adjust, you'll never stop making progress.

Remember when I mentioned that 9 out of 10 of my ads fail?

Yeah, that's not an exaggeration. That is likely what will happen in your case too.

I know, I know, every other "coaching program" out there wants to make it seem super easy to find that winner. But it's not.

It's simple, but not easy.

However, it really only takes a few minutes per day to evaluate your content and make adjustments.

When you make adjustments, you'll use what I call the **7-Day Flywheel System.**

The Flywheel allows you to consistently optimize your content in order to maintain very low cost. Now everything will be more profitable!

By the end of this chapter you will have complete clarity on where to look to evaluate your content **and** you'll know how to fix it.

The 7-Day Flywheel system gets the losers out as quickly as possible so you can find the winners and put them to work for you.

YOUR FIRST 7-DAY CONTENT FLYWHEEL

Right now, your ecosystem should look like this.

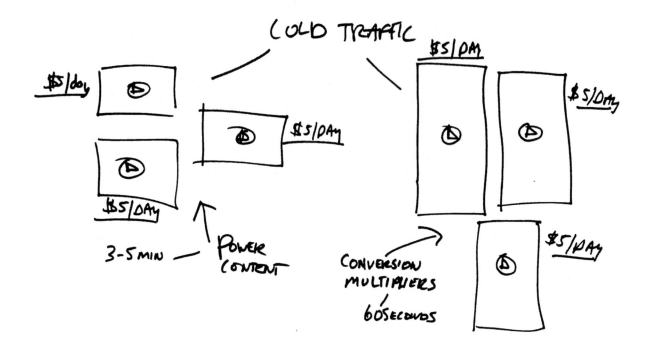

After the initial launch is where a lot of my students like to sit on their hands and just wait. But that's not how you get paid! Don't hesitate for a moment!

I can't stress this enough: Don't post an ad and then sit on your ass and wait a month!

I'm not trying to be mean here. I just know that if you take that route, you won't find the results you're looking for, and I want you to succeed!

The first thing to optimize is your Tier 1 content that goes to **cold** traffic. This is the Top of Funnel (TOF).

We want to bring in those invisible leads as quickly as possible.

To do that, you've gotta start putting out new content.

Here's an example step-by-step of what your **first** 7-day Content Flywheel looks like in action.

Day 1: Check power content metrics, kill any that aren't working

Day 2: Check conversion multiplier metrics, kill any that aren't working

Day 3: Produce a new power content video and launch it to cold traffic

Day 4: Produce a new conversion multiplier video and launch it to cold traffic

Day 5: Produce a new power content video and launch it to cold traffic

Day 6: Produce a new conversion multiplier video and launch it to cold traffic

Day 7: Produce a new power content video and launch it to cold traffic

Here is a snapshot of me doing the process for those of you who are visual like me.

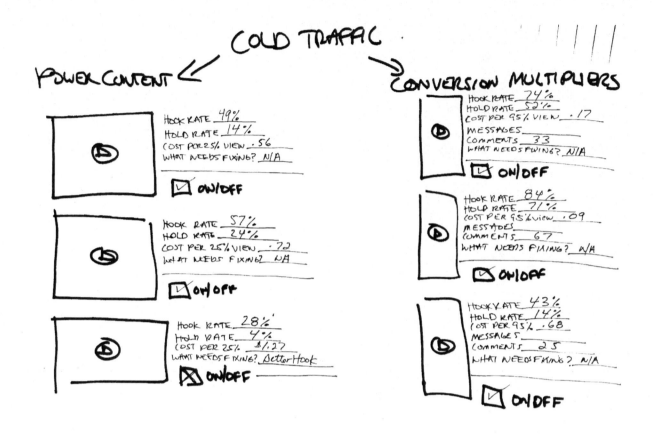

COLD TRAFFIC

POWER CONTENT

HOOK RATE __49%__
HOLD RATE __14%__
COST PER 25% VIEW __.56__
WHAT NEEDS FIXING? __N/A__

☑ ON/OFF

HOOK RATE __57%__
HOLD RATE __24%__
COST PER 25% VIEW __.72__
WHAT NEEDS FIXING? __N/A__

☑ ON/OFF

HOOK RATE __28%__
HOLD RATE __4%__
COST PER 25% __$1.27__
WHAT NEEDS FIXING? __Better Hook__
☒ ON/OFF

CONVERSION MULTIPLIERS

HOOK RATE __74%__
HOLD RATE __52%__
COST PER 95% VIEW __.17__
MESSAGES __
COMMENTS __33__
WHAT NEEDS FIXING? __N/A__

☑ ON/OFF

HOOK RATE __84%__
HOLD RATE __71%__
COST PER 95% view __.09__
MESSAGES __
COMMENTS __67__
WHAT NEEDS FIXING? __N/A__

☑ ON/OFF

HOOK RATE __43%__
HOLD RATE __14%__
COST PER 95% __.68__
MESSAGES __
COMMENTS __25__
WHAT NEEDS FIXING? __N/A__

☑ ON/OFF

IMPORTANT - Repeat this Flywheel every 7 days until you have 3 power content videos producing invisible leads for under $1 **and** you have at least 1,000 people on your Invisible List.

I'm also checking that my conversion multipliers are collectively bringing in at least 100 messenger conversations of the right people each week.

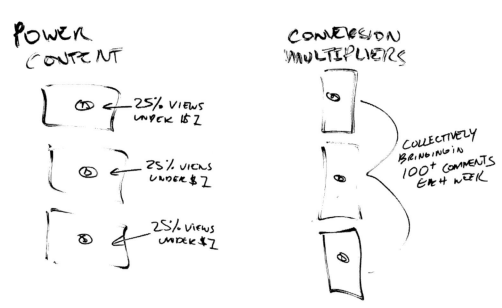

At the end of the chapter I'll give you an on-going checklist that you can use **after** you've built your Invisible List to over 1,000 members.

Next up, I need to show you how to know if your ads are hitting the mark, or as we call them in the marketing world… Key Performance Indicators (KPIs)

IS YOUR CONTENT WORKING?

The three KPIs we track for TOF, to make sure we're putting out the right video content to attract our ideal clients are:

1. **HOOK RATE** - this measures the % of people who are stopping the scroll

2. **HOLD RATE** - this measures the % of people who watch at least 15 seconds of your content

3. **COST PER Video View** - this measures how many people viewed a certain % of your video.

Getting both of these KPIs involves a little math but I think you can handle it.

Hook Rate = 3 second video views divided by the number of impressions. You'll want to keep this **above 40%.**

Hold Rate - 15 second video views divided by the number of impressions. If you get at least 8%-10% here, you are in good shape.

Cost per video view (Power Content) = total ad spend divided by number of 25% video views. You want to keep the cost below $1 for a 25% video view.

Cost per video view (Conversion Multiplier) = total ad spend divided by number of 95% video views. You want to keep the cost below $1 for a 95% video view.

Take a look at this screenshot of some Power Content from my ads manager:

Ad	Hook Rate	Hold Rate	Cost per ThruPlay	Cost Per 25% View	CTR (all)
70% Call Price	48.48%	8.84%	$0.03	0.45	0.91%
$500/mo video funnel funnel	48.94%	7.39%	$0.04	0.94	0.35%
The $10/Day Funnel	48.70%	9.84%	$0.03	—	0.52%
Results from 3 ads ⓘ	**48.70%**	**8.82%**	**$0.03** Per Action	**0.95**	**0.60%** Per Impressions

See those Hook Rates? Over 40%.

Now look at the cost per 25% view. Less than $1.

That means, these ads are performing at the rate they should be.

When an ad performs as it should, we keep it running because it is building our invisible list in a hyper cost-effective way. Remember, the invisible list from Chapter 3? Tracking KPI's and adjusting is the method to ensure that your invisible list is growing.

Remember, these KPI's are for measuring your Power Content and Conversion Multipliers that you are delivering to a cold audience. They are for your Top Of Funnel.

Let's break down each one of these and talk about how to improve each metric if they are not performing.

Grab an over-the-shoulder view of how to set these custom metrics up in ads manager here:

www.adswithlaurel.com/metricsetup

IMPROVING HOOK RATE

If your Hook Rate is less than 40%, there are two primary culprits.

One is that your audience is off. This is rarely the case, but it's where most people focus their energy. Instead, the more likely culprit is that **your hook isn't specific enough**. It's too vague, so your audience ignores it and moves on.

It almost always comes down to the hook!

The hook needs to be clear on **WHO** the content is for and **WHY** they would want to watch the video. It needs to be a "dog whistle."

For real, like bleeding ears kinda dog whistle. Don't be subtle.

Let's pretend that I take everyone who buys my book to Disneyland for a bonus trip. (*I'm so fun, right?*)

And as soon as all of us walk through the gate, you all take off to different sides of the park.

Some of you run off to Space Mountain…

Some of you run off to Thunder Railroad…

Some of you run to Cinderella's Castle…

But you guys all forgot your Genie Passes that get you to the front of the line for any ride!

So I SHOUT AS LOUD AS I CAN…

"HEY… FOR THOSE OF YOU WHO BOUGHT SUPER DUPER PROFITABLE ADS FROM LAUREL, I HAVE YOUR GENIE PASSES!"

You guys will all immediately come to a halt, turn around and then immediately run back to grab those passes, right?

Well, **most** of you would.

Some of you will ignore me and just keep going… and we will get some "Looky Loos" who will also turn around, but **MOST** of my people will come running to me.

THAT is how strong your hook should be.

Sure, you'll attract some who aren't your audience, but for the most part, you'll attract the peeps who are your tribe.

With content, a lot of experts tend to stay too broad in their hook.

For example:

"Coaches and consultants who have an ad problem."

That's not very specific, is it?

But what if I said, "Coaches who want to book more calls, don't use **THIS** ad strategy."

See the difference?

I bet a lot of my ideal clients turn around and watch that video *(by the way that is by far my most successful hook I've ever used).*

As much as we want people to watch our video, we also want to make sure it's the *right* people.

If your hook rate is under 40%, take a look at your hook!

Adjust your hook to be *more* specific and don't forget that dog whistle shout-out!

IMPROVING HOLD RATE

I want all videos to hit at least 8-10% hold rate. The way to measure this is to divide your 15 second video views (thruplays) by the amount of impressions.

So if I have 1,000 impressions and 57 people have watched my video for at least 15 seconds, we will do the following math.

$57/1{,}000 = .057 \times 100 = 5.7\%$

If your hold rate is less than 8%, one, two, or all of the following is likely the case.

1. You introduced yourself too much
2. The promise of value wasn't strong
3. You try to solve too big of a problem within one piece of content (this one also affects cost per video view)

Experts love to toot their own horn, but some of us like to do it a little too much. When you introduce yourself, it should be 2-3 sentences *max* in these content pieces. With cold traffic, we can't leave it out completely, because then they won't know who we are! But it's gotta be short and sweet to keep their attention.

The humble brag is a little nuance that people miss, but it's some of the most important lines in the process. If you've already forgotten what this is, go back to Chapter 4 for a quick review.

Here's my favorite example from one of my videos (hehe, that was sort of a humble brag about my humble brag).

"My name is Laurel Portié, the owner of adcoachingfor7.com where I have now taught over 10,000 business owners how to launch simple $5 ads to grow their business."

Notice, I worked a *lot* of important things into that one single sentence.

1. My name
2. My vanity URL
3. Social Proof
4. My specialty

The second issue with hold rate is that the promise of value isn't strong enough or not present at all.

This was a little trick I learned in television while promoting the 11pm news. If I told my audience that in the next 3 minutes they would learn XYZ, I could hold them through that commercial break.

The promise of value plays an equally important role in our content, **ESPECIALLY** to cold traffic. Someone might not sit through a video no matter how short it is if they don't know you. That's why it's important that we hook them by telling them "In the next 60 seconds you'll learn X" or "In the next 3 minutes i'll show you X."

The third issue is when you try to solve too big of a problem with a single piece of content. I see this all the time. My students want to promote things like "How to go from zero to 6 figures in 90 days" or "How to lose 30 pounds over the next 3 months."

While those **are** specific solutions people are looking for... we want to help them get over a single hurdle this week.

When you are dealing with cold traffic, you have to assume that they are also seeing other ads and messages from other sources. If your big promise sounds the same as everyone else's, you're more likely to get ignored.

Instead of helping someone go from "zero to 6 figures in 90 days"... break down a small problem in their client acquisition system that they can solve as fast as possible.

For example, you could say "Send this 1 email today to book 2-10 appointments on your calendar this week."

Pause here. Can you tell the difference?!

Can you *feel* the difference?

Notice how concrete that is. I'm talking about **one** e-mail. Then a **specific** number of new appointments. It's so much more powerful as a single piece of content than making larger than life claims that people have heard 100 times before.

When you frame your hooks this way, you immediately stand out above the noise.

Here's another good example, "My clients ate only these 8 foods and lost on average 5 pounds this week."

Compare that to "lose 30 pounds in 3 weeks" and it's clear why it's the winner. It's clear, specific, and aims at a quick win in a short time frame rather than solving everything all at once.

Once you get your Hook Rate and Hold Rate up to standard, it's time to turn your attention to the most important variable: Cost per video view.

IMPROVING COST PER VIDEO VIEW

At the Top of your Funnel (TOF) you will have both Power Content videos and Conversion Multipliers. For this KPI, we calculate each metric separately.

For TOF Power Content, the goal is $1 or less per 25% view. The way to measure this is to divide the cost of the total adspend by the number of 25% video views.

So if I spent $5/day for 7 days on one ad, that's $35 total for that time period. And let's say during that time period, I had 42 people who viewed at least 25% of that video. The equation would look like this...

$35/42 = $.83/video view.

For your Conversion Multipliers, the math is the same, except we only consider those who watch at least 95% of the video because they are so much shorter.

So if I spent $5/day for 7 days and had 42 people who watched at least 95% of that Conversion Multiplier, then I would get the same metric. 83 cents per video view.

In both examples, our hypothetical video hits the KPI we want, so we keep it.

These are by far the **HARDEST** metric to hit. Whether your video is 60 seconds or 3 minutes, getting people to watch for an entire minute is challenging, *especially cold traffic.*

If you're not getting under $1 per video view, there are 3 likely causes:

1. You took too long to get the point
2. You didn't deliver on your promise
3. The content fell short

Let's break these down a bit.

You'll notice that the first issue is closely related to Hook Rate and Hold Rate performance. If you take too long to get to the point, even if someone happens to watch beyond 15 seconds, it's unlikely they will stick around for the whole thing.

So even if your Hook Rate and Hold Rate are on target, this is still your best first level of intervention. Your introduction should be a **really** tight script that you can confidently recite on the spot.

Write out your introduction and remove **anything** that isn't absolutely necessary.

Second, you have to evaluate if you delivered on your promise. If you promise to give someone the one tactic to help them get xyz in the next week, you have to ask yourself: *"Did I actually clearly explain that one tactic and give them an action step?"* **OR**, you might evaluate whether or not you clearly explained how they can get the value bomb that helps them activate that one tactic.

This one is usually pretty easy to self-diagnose if you are brutally honest with yourself. If your KPI's aren't on track, review your video content and do **not** be kind to yourself.

Finally, the content might just be falling short. This means that for some reason the message isn't resonating with your audience.

More often than not, you are offering something that your audience simply isn't interested in.

I'll give you another fitness niche example here. Let's say you want to target people who want to lose weight. But then you publish a piece of Power Content that explains proper form for the barbell deadlift.

Think about it. Most exercisers who just want to lose weight couldn't care less about the nuances of deadlift technique. And most folks who want to improve specifically deadlift technique probably aren't too concerned with weight loss.

So you have to ask yourself…

Does my educational content align with what my audience feels to be their most immediate need?

This one can be tricky to diagnose, but when you slow down and put yourself in your prospect's shoes, it's likely you'll find an immediate need around which you can create content.

SWIPE MY PERSONAL METRICS SHEET BELOW

Below is the sheet that I personally used **EVERY** week until **EVERY** Power Content video was hitting video view KPIs. It also helped me ensure that my Conversion Multipliers were bringing in at least 100 messenger conversations.

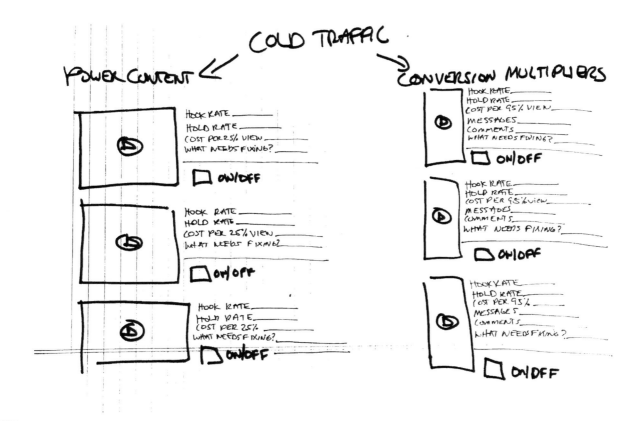

You can grab a PDF of this graphic at
www.adswithlaurel.com/metrics

DEVELOPING YOUR 2ND TIER

The next tier of content is your Middle of Funnel (MOF). This includes your Power Content **with** Call to Action (CTA) and your next layer of Conversion Multipliers. These have only one variable to track…

How many people are commenting to request your value bomb.

Keep in mind, this is **very** different than tracking a specific KPI within your ads manager.

Here's what it looks like:

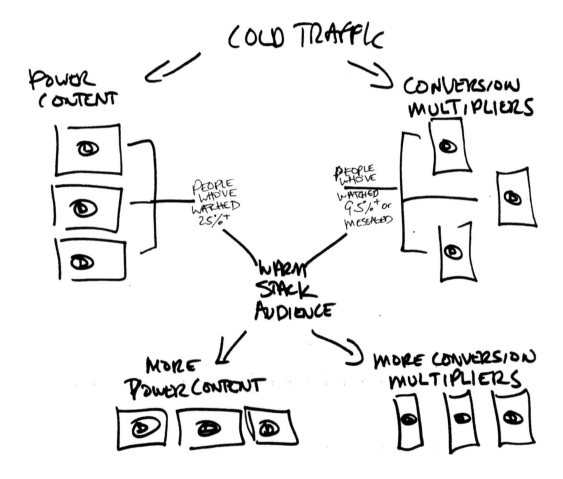

This "Warm Stack Audience" is the Invisible List you've been building. This content won't get delivered to your Invisible List until you've got at least 1,000 people in that audience, but that won't stop us from getting it published right away.

You'll notice from the diagram that the 2nd Tier has Power Content as well as more Conversion Multipliers.

Each type of content will have a Call to Action (CTA). However, there is an important distinction between these two types of call to action!

In your **Conversion Multipliers**, the 60-second short form video, your call to action is asking people to respond if they want the value bomb you are offering.

But with your **Tier 2 Power Content,** the call to action will be an invitation to work with you.

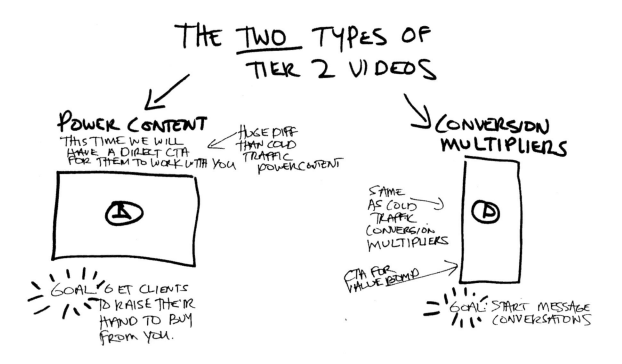

For example, in a Conversion Multiplier, I might say "comment YES below if you'd like me to send you the cheat sheet on how to launch your first ad."

But for the 2nd Tier Power Content, the call to action could be "If you'd like for me to show you what this strategy would look like for your business, drop me a line below this video and I'll reach out and we can hop on a quick zoom call and I'll give you a free demo."

Both calls to action invite a conversation in Messenger, but each one sets different expectations for the prospect.

A common question I get at this stage is…

"Laurel, why are we **ONLY** asking people to work with us in the Tier 2 Power Content and not anywhere else?"

Remember something called Pipeline Equity that I taught you back in an earlier chapter? We want to keep our content ratio 75% goodwill content and 25% sales content. The Tier 2 Power Content is where we will actually pitch them at the end of our value video to work with us.

I told you this strategy is *super stealth!*

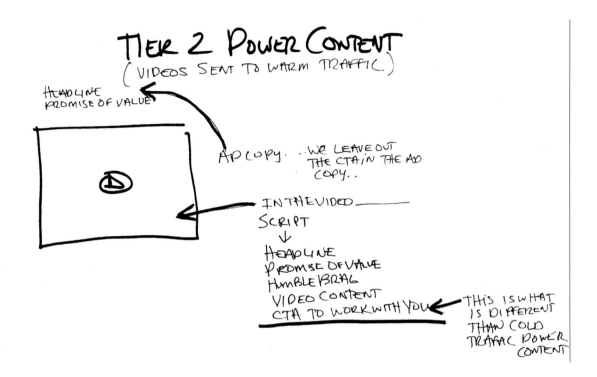

While we're on the topic of direct offers, I want to highlight how simple the invitation can be.

Take a look at my example again. "If you'd like for me to show you what this strategy would look like for your business, drop me a line below this video and I'll reach out and we can hop on a quick zoom call and I'll give you a free demo."

I know that a little purple book told you that you need to make one very strong promise along with a guarantee that will make your offer "irresistible."

I am going to challenge that right now.

What if I told you that I made my first million **WITHOUT** having a one sentence "irresistible offer?"

That's exactly what I did, and it's my macro-belief that **POSITIONING** is **way** more important than an offer.

What do I mean by positioning?

Market positioning refers to the ability to influence consumer perception regarding a brand or product relative to competitors. The objective of market positioning is to establish the image or identity of a brand or product so that consumers perceive it in a certain way (credit for this definition - corporatefinanceinsitute.com)

To give you a clear concrete example.

In the beginning of this book, I told you guys about the start of my business. I went LIVE for over 100 days teaching business owners how to do a simple $5 ad strategy.

I never put out any promises or guarantees.

Everyday, I showed them over-the-shoulder examples of what I was doing and proof of results from ad manager screenshots and the recorded zoom calls I was doing with happy customers.

I never had to sell my "offer."

My audience already knew the value I could bring from me showing up and giving them an over-the-shoulder look at what I was doing and the results I was getting.

They saw my content and said, "I want **THAT!**"

How much easier do you think it is to sell your program and services when people are asking you... "How do I work with you?"

I don't think I have to explain how much easier it is. You're a smart cookie.

After you've launched everything, you should have:

1. 3 Power Content Videos in Tier 1 of your funnel

2. 3 Conversion Multipliers in Tier 1 of your funnel

3. A mix of Power Content *with* CTA and Conversion Multipliers in Tier 2 of your funnel

Once all of that is in place, here's what your completed funnel looks like. You'll notice that **MOST** of the ecosystem is built to start conversations while one part goes after a direct sale.

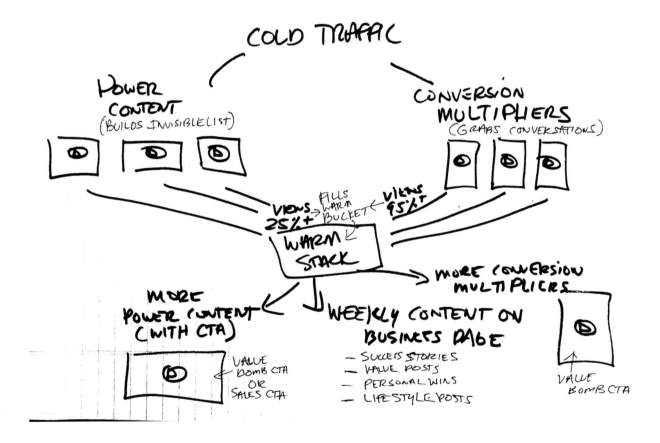

Ad Budget:

$5/day per Power Content video to COLD traffic

$5/day per Conversion Multiplier to COLD traffic

$2/day per Power Content video to WARM traffic

$2/day per Power Content video to WARM traffic

TEST AND RETEST

Here's one example of how this can play out in real life.

A new client of mine needed to have conversations to get feedback on a new offer…

So, I helped her create a value bomb that would attract who she thought was her ideal client then helped her write a 60 second reels ad to give it away.

We threw it into ads manager for $5/day.

On the 1st day, she had 34 people raise their hand to say "I want that thing..."

To everyone that said "I want that thing," I helped her craft this **EXACT DM.**

"Hey X. I see you want my guide to X.

I actually have two versions of it.

Are you _____ or _____?

How you answer that will determine which I give you."

The result?

16 people ghosted

18 people responded

0 of the 18 people actually needed that specific value bomb

11 of the 18 people weren't ready for that value bomb, so I helped her create another on the spot and delivered it

So I helped her write a new 60 second reel to give away THAT value bomb and the next day I helped her launch a new 60 second reels ad to give that new value bomb away...

This time she got…

86 hand raises

We tweaked the DM script to reflect the changes

"Hey X. I see you want my guide to X.

I actually have two versions of it.

Are you _____ or _____?

How you answer that will determine which I give you.

Now this was the result.

11 people ghosted her.

75 people responded.
She was able to transition 2 of those to a phone call and now I'm going to work with her on transitioning those leads into more phone calls.

We are also going to double down and spend $10/day on this ad to get more volume because now we know it works!

IMPROVING VALUE BOMBS

When you are not getting the comments you want on your value bomb offer, it's likely due to two major causes:

1. People aren't ready for that value bomb (like in the example above)

2. The value bomb isn't connected to the prospect's felt need

This is why starting real conversations with prospects is so vital, ***especially*** when you are first starting out with your paid ad campaigns.

The fix on this one is simple. If no one comments to request your value bomb in your 2nd Tier Content, offer a new value bomb!

I know, that sounds too easy, right?

But remember, you are speaking to people from your invisible list who have already watched at least 25% of your Power Content and 95% or more of your Conversion Multipliers. So while they might not be super warm yet, they are warm enough to respond if the value bomb is relevant to them.

A BONUS TO GIVE YOU A BOOST

Take another look at that diagram above. You'll notice I snuck in a little something extra.

The #1 complaint I get from students is that their organic reach on their business page sucks.

So here's your **bonus...**

Any time I post content on my business page, whether it's success stories, value posts I write out with text, a personal win or any fun lifestyle posts I simply "Boost" that content to that Invisible List audience that I am using to send my tier 2 content to.

You're welcome!

Ad Budget
$3/10 days for Boosted Posts to your business page content

WHY I DON'T MEASURE RETARGETING METRICS

Throughout this entire book, I have laid out a few fun stories that I learned from working in television. The way my brain thinks about retargeting also comes from those good ole days at CBS.

You see, I've never had a client come in and demand to know "which commercial brought in that client?" That actually sounds pretty silly when you think of it that way, right?

Yet, so many of us want to treat the social media ads platform in exactly that way. I hope that by reading this book, you no longer see the platform as a slot machine, getting X amount of dollars back from whatever dollar amount you're putting in. Instead, I hope by now you have started to see that advertising isn't one dimensional.

I often get asked the question…

"Laurel, what metrics do you read when it comes to retargeting?"

I say, "I don't even look at the metrics, at least not in the way that we do for the cold traffic campaigns."

Let me explain what I mean by that.

Let's say you see one of my Power Content ads and you watch it 25% but you don't ask for my value bomb.

The next day, you're retargeted by one of my conversion multiplier ads. You see it, but you don't even watch it… you just keep scrolling.

Over a period of the next 4 months, you see my content show up in your newsfeed consistently.

You watch my videos, but never comment until one day you see one of my longer form tier 2 power content videos and you take me up on my offer to book a free strategy call with me.

Which of those ads worked?

Come on, you know the answer to that by now.

They **ALL** worked.

But the ads platform will only show the conversion on the Tier 2 Power Content video ad. This is why you cannot look at ads as one dimensional. Just like why my television commercial clients never asked me… "Which commercial brought in those sales?"

YOUR ON-GOING 7-DAY CONTENT FLYWHEEL

Now that you've got everything in place, it's just a matter of constant practice and repetition of the basics.

This is what I have done **every** single day over the last 5 years. This is the **SECRET** to going from zero to almost $3 million in sales in just a few years.

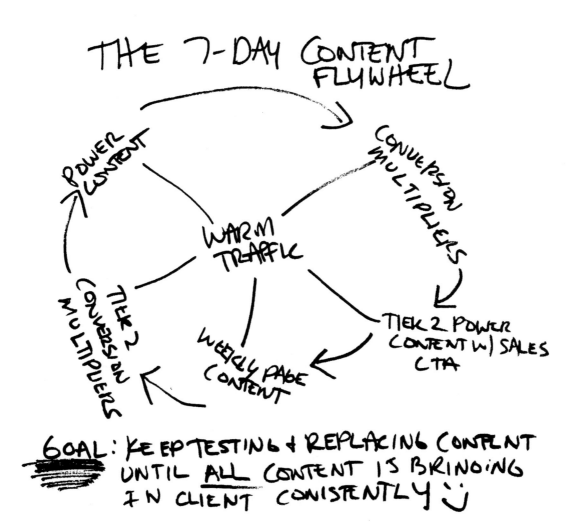

Here's how it plays out...

Day 1: Check Power Content cold traffic content metrics, kill any that aren't working

Day 2: Check cold traffic Conversion Multiplier metrics, kill any that aren't working

Day 3: Post a piece of content on business page

Day 4: Produce a new Power Content video and launch it to cold traffic

Day 5: Post a piece of content on business page

Day 6: Replace any cold traffic Power Content videos with new ones to test

Day 7: Replace any cold traffic Conversion Multipliers that aren't working

Day 8: Start the flywheel over

IMPORTANT - This is the Flywheel you'll use *after* you've reached at least 1,000 people in your Invisible List.

To see this in action and download the checklist for your 7-Day Flywheel, click the link below:

www.adswithlaurel.com/checklist

The video highlights the Content Flywheel principle, which is to take consistent action, always test your content, and continue to always optimize. Most folks post some ads and then sit on them for a month waiting for stats. That's not the approach here!

Get that content up and then continue adding new content and optimizing.

THE WRAP-UP
WHY MY $5 ADS ECOSYSTEM IS FAIL-PROOF

You made it! The most common feedback I get from students after they go through this material for the first time is, "That was amazing! But I still don't think I understand it all the way."

And that's okay!

You don't need to understand **everything** perfectly the first time through.

Because there's one little secret to success that you may have already figured out by this point.

You see, most of my competitors ran ads for…

7 days — *then gave up*
30 days — *then gave up*
60 days — *then gave up*
90 days — *then gave up*

And now, over 5 years later, I'm one of the **ONLY** people still running ads to the **SAME** offer.

For those who've been following me for a while, they can observe that most of my competitors have dropped off and now they see me as the **ONLY** option.

I may not be the "*best*" at ads, but I am the one who has stalked my audience the longest.

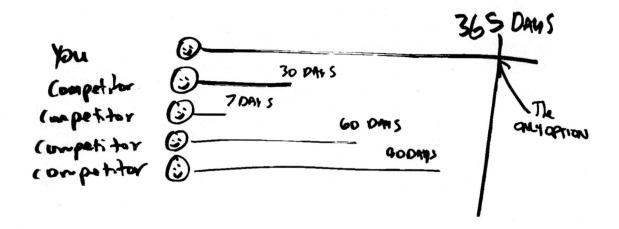

In this book, I really wanted to give you the big picture perspective and pull back the curtain on everything, so you know exactly what you'll be **implementing** when you join my $7 program.

If you're new to this game, there's a lot to learn, but the great news is that it's something that anyone **CAN** learn with the right guidance.

Simply by reading this book, you are already lightyears ahead of most of the coaches and service providers out there.

But wherever you are in this process, I want to personally invite you to join the community of thousands of other entrepreneurs just like you who are putting this stuff into play and getting amazing results.

https://www.adcoachingfor7.com/

Inside the community you'll get personalized feedback on your ads as well as fresh content every single month to help you consistently implement this strategy.

Developing mastery over this strategy might take a few months to really hone in, depending on how much time you spend with it.

But the more you think on it, and mentally wrestle with it, the deeper it will burrow into your brain and eventually become second nature to you.

I'll leave you with this -- before you close this book (or the tab it's opened in), make sure you take just **ONE** action, based on your starting point.

It might be to sit down and actually write down what your offer is.

It might be to record your first live video.

It might be digging into ads manager and running your first video views campaign.

The point is, nothing happens without the first step. And the first step is the thing that most people hesitate on.

But you don't have to be "most people" today.

You can choose to rise above.

You can take an action today you've never taken before.

You can leap into uncertainty even though it's unfamiliar.

You can create a new reality.

And if you need some help along the way, you know where to find me.

I AM NOBODY SPECIAL...
I WORKED A FULL TIME JOB AND
BUILT THIS BUSINESS IN MY OWN
FREE TIME.

VIDEOS GOT ME TO WHERE I AM
TODAY.

I HOPE THIS PLAYBOOK SERVES
YOU THE SAME WAY IT HAS
SERVED ME.

ADDITIONAL RESOURCES AND TRAINING IN THIS BOOK

My YouTube Channel

www.youtube.com/thelaurelshow

Power Content Creation Workshop

www.adswithlaurel.com/powercontent

Messenger Framework to Create Conversations

www.adswithlaurel.com/messenger

$500/month Ad Strategy Workshop

www.adswithlaurel.com/500

Ad Manager Setup

www.adswithlaurel.com/setups

Custom Ad Metrics Setup

www.adswithlaurel.com/metricsetup

Daily Checklist + Content Flywheel

www.adswithlaurel.com/checklist

Value Bomb Workshop

adswithlaurel.com/valuebombs

Laurel's Personal Metrics PDF

www.adswithlaurel.com/metrics

WAYS TO WORK WITH ME

Personalized Help and Support for your Ads

https://www.adcoachingfor7.com/

Lean on Laurel

www.adswithlaurel.com

Made in United States
North Haven, CT
20 April 2024

51560011R00070